Wilderness Places
The Underbrush of Life's Journey

Marche H. Singleton

Kingdom Builders Publications LLC

Wilderness Places: The Underbrush of Life's Journey

© 2020 Marche H. Singleton
Kingdom Builders Publications

All rights reserved. No part of this book may be reproduced or transmitted in any form or by any means without written permission from the author.

Second Edition

Printed in the USA
SOFT COVER ISBN: 978-0-578-64634-3
Library of Congress Control Number: 2020909196

Authored by Marche H. Singleton

Edited by
Editor-in-chief Wanda Brown
Louise James
Kingdom Builders Publications

Photographer
Michael Singleton

Cover Design
LoMar Designs

Contact information:
msingl5289@yahoo.com
kbpublications@outlook.com

This Book Belongs to

DEDICATION

It is said that it takes a village to raise a child and as I took a review of my life, I believe that proved to be true. Because this book is a house for short stories that recall times of this little girl, once broken but repaired. It is befitting that the village gets a little mention.

To the hard workers who set the tone of a work ethic, and the alcoholics who encouraged me to stay in school and never drink. To the entire neighborhood of Washington Park, located in Fayetteville, NC., as the Shirelles best said it in a song, "*This is dedicated to the one I love.*" It was a neighborhood formed of dirt streets, no streetlights, out houses and pumps for water. It sounds like the intro sentence of a poverty filled story but it was not. It was a neighborhood, a village steeped in rich nutrients of life lessons necessary for my survival.

A special thanks to Richard and Rosa Evans who allowed me a special place in their family tree. Richard Evans and Oscar Smith were my two fathers; not connected by DNA, but reserved with a special love in my heart. To the Jenkins family and their son Richard Jenkins, the veteran. It may have appeared that he was lost after his call of duty but his thoughtfulness served to save me and my children on several occasions. So thank you Mr. Jenkins for my porch food. The families who shaped my life and heart are plenty and for all of them I give thanks.

The most special thanks will also be reserved for Irene Ingram also known as my Aunt Sis-Rena or Grandma Nina, named by my daughter because she couldn't pronounce the whole name as a child. My children, Wandra, Richard and Michael, their children, and their children's children. That special group proved to be the wind beneath my wings. But it was Aunt Sis Rena who repaired my wings so I could fly. May she rest in peace as I remain ever grateful to her.

Endless love…

CONTENTS

	Dedication	iv
	Preface	viii
	Introduction	xi
1	A Broken Seed	14
2	Innocence Lost	33
3	Until Death Do We Part	45
4	Seventy-Two Hour Notice	57
5	Death and Taxes	70
6	Obedience is Better that Sacrifice	77
7	Employment Woes	84
8	Porch Food	96
9	A Someday Place	103
10	The End of a Season	111
	More About the Author	114

PREFACE

You won't find wilderness places on a road map; however you can recognize them after you've lived through a few of them during your own life's travel. With a dash of hindsight and a bag of developed faith, you will be more able to see your growth and development as you've moved from one place to another.

For me, one was found in a hospital with a grandchild, delivered in a maternity ward, then taken to the hospital morgue. Other places were picked up in corridors of criminal court rooms and released after that boy developed into a man they said would never live to be.

Yet another place was found in a smile when the mother-daughter madness delivered us from a place of turmoil to a place called friendship. Others were like waters that ran into bathtubs attempting to wash away dirtiness of a rape and dried off accidentally when looking for relief from something else. Then, moving into divorce of a husband whom I didn't think I would outlive. I could not match the sorrow in a child's heart when the news pronounced, "Your father committed suicide last night." Oh, the suicide of a genius loved-one who would never know what beauty he cheated his son and the world out of.

Then there's the ringing of fire trucks that came to put out a house fire, but were too late to save much, still I was able to walk away with everything that was essential, my life. Yes, I was still standing alive around the ashes of items that once represented my entire life.

As sad and painful as many of these places proved to be, inside each place was a glue that promised to hold things together and help me keep a necessary amount of daily sanity which was required for living out my days. That glue traveled with me to complete a college degree while completing daily commutes out of a neighborhood deemed to be one of New York's most dangerous. The sustaining glue got me through buying flowers for a son's prom merely months after the father's funeral.

The list of wilderness places could match tall mountains and like tall mountains there was a sun that always shined above my head with a promise of better days. I chose to call that light God. This would not be the type of God found only on Easter morning with the Sunday best dress, or the church service that requires the speaking in tongues or the type of church commitment that provides you privilege to sit in the front pews. No, but it is the type of God that you hear in the rush of a wave or taste when the salt of the ocean spills upon your mouth. It is that God you can feel when the sun is so hot it burns into your skin and suddenly this wonderful breeze blows and it's even more wonderful because you can't see where it came from. That is the glue…this is the God who stood between every second sanity was slipping from my mind, but I kept still so I would not follow that moment into the rabbit hole.

The religious experiences I've had between Methodist, Catholic. and Baptist churches taught me that the routines of religions often bind souls to a ritual while discarding the very essence of a relationship between me and the Creator. I am grateful that even in the crazy happening in my days, the idea of connecting to a Creator that made water wet, or dirt dry makes me feel some special kind of way. I suppose life brings wilderness places to each one of us. I said to a neighbor once that I believe I receive these places like mail addressed to "occupant" but the mailman stopped dropping off those notices at my door. The truth is all the living will receive that mail one day or another.

No matter what you do, the wilderness of life is unavoidable. The important thing to remember is you will work your way out. As my grandmother used to say, "Trouble don't last always." In the meantime you must be an active participant in your removal and diligent about the exit.

My life's journeys have placed me often, as another neighbor of mine would say, at the "hind wheels of bad luck." Fortunately for me that wheel was round and it did keep turning. That will be the case with us all.

INTRODUCTION

Wilderness places, not a forest of trees but an accumulation of underbrush, aka life's problems. This place is the only place where the presence of every human being will be found on one day or another. Exception is not provided in exchange of great wealth nor will the cry of poverty provide a day pass. Life's problems will become a travel partner and reckoning will be required by all. That truth sounds a bit intimidating but truth be told, it won't be if you don't let it be.

This book is a series of three layouts, one story at a time, details of different life problems I searched answers for. The suspect subjects are the typical, health, finances, depression, rejection, responsibility, expectations, and the list goes on. While all problems have solutions or acceptance required, problems expand tenfold when they come with answers we are not prepared to accept. When my husband committed suicide or when we lost the grandchild who was not even one day old, there were no solutions. Acceptance was required. No amount of explanations of why babies die as soon as they are born, or how depression can lead to suicide would alter those facts. There lies the true making of wilderness places. Then there are the regular everyday issues which rose out of DNA, gender, race, and the many rules which define or restrict, request permission, or seek approval for participation. None of these may be the hand requested but the hand dealt. When the employer has used you for two hours of interviewing only to say, we can't hire you because you're Black, the underbrush swallows you up. Right or wrong, I was still unemployed and had to back bench a piece of realty for a later day of depression. Unlike a forest with real trees you can walk around them and continue your journey. However, the underbrush, what these problems become, is not always easily nor quickly maneuvered through. If you are not careful you can get stuck there wasting time trying to clear a path. This is the hand of unacceptance.

The more I wrote down my problems and experienced a private party of reminiscing, I witnessed a pattern. Problems came. I was slowed down in my tracks by worry, depression, and fear. I then looked outward for help. Over the years, I discovered my move-out speed increased, pushed on by assurance. If I could get over yesterday, I would probably get over tomorrow so I kept it moving.

As I sat typing up some of the last words for this book my grandson asked me, what kind of book was I writing? I said it was an inspirational book. I only pray that reading my stories will provide people with a hope. I remind myself; I've got at least forty years or more worth of living, writing, and learning. It has brought me to book publication. Nothing happened over night apparently there was a lot to learn.

As my grandmother said, "Trouble don't last always." When trouble passes don't rest there in despair. Accept unwelcomed outcomes or you will become a piece of something never to realize your whole. There are situations that hurt to the core and you're certain you will never recover, but what would be the good in that. It wouldn't change the facts but what it would change is your opportunity to make your mark. I do not believe our lives are some random act of errors. We are born with great potential and purpose even if we do grow out of different gardens. With this potential and purpose we could light up the darkness when we commit to living our best lives and be joy seekers in the interim. It serves no one to simmer in sorrow or depression or disappointments. Life is for the living and we should live.

Although I didn't paten the phrase, "life is good", I believe it to be true. Life does happen and it is good and not good, but there is so much joy to be had we should be busy beavers seeking it. I hope you find through the pages of my book, **Wilderness Places**. I had some troubles, I got over them and I exited my wilderness places in time enough to still find some peace and joy. This I hope for you as well.

Peace.

A BROKEN SEED
Chapter One

Initially, my life's journey started out on a path that appeared to have been ruled by simplicity. Life was simple and from the heart of a five-year-old it appeared to be quite good and simple without any hint of change ever. Sundays were highly responsible for that life forecast. For as long as I could remember, almost a whole five years, Sundays were filled with the aromas of meat loaf, banana pudding (all made from scratch) and some vegetables I wouldn't want to remember. My mother's attentions were always in the living room with my stepfather where loud shouts of baseball calls could be heard. The loudness of baseball fans served to drown out the rambling sounds I made opening pots and undoing foil-covered dishes. I would routinely steal hands full of my favorite two foods and run off to my private place, the bathroom, to enjoy my feast.

The bathroom was and remains the one place in most houses where respect is distributed to all family members equally, one knock, "you in there?" A reply of yes and whoever knocked either yells for you to hurry up or walks away satisfied of your whereabouts. But never, would anyone just barge in. So that kept it safe for me to sit inside the huge claw leg bathtub with my stolen food of banana pudding and meat loaf and enjoy every bite. Upon completion of my feast I would wash my hands, after all I did use the bathroom, and wait the next several hours for my real dinner.

Then there were my older brothers whom I had mastered crying for on demand. This was used to encourage my mother to make them take me to the movies on Sunday afternoons after the real dinner. They would comply or at least in front of her. Then they would take me to the scariest movie ever and I would either, 1) have the worst nightmare or, 2) not ask them to take me again for a while. Life was good by the time I was five years old and I had no indication that it would ever change.

We lived in a two-story house in Philadelphia where we could stand on the roof tops safely and watch the annual parades. My stepfather, who I could only remember as Mr. Brooks, was my partner in my nighttime step game. He would sit on the steps blocking my passage up to my room until he tickled me sufficiently or rubbed his beard against my face until I giggled helplessly. I could never remember if he was tall or short, thin, or fat but I remember him as love. He was kind and brought a certain kind of light with him that made me feel all right. It didn't matter whether my brothers took me with them or not because I would always have Sunday dinners, a stepfather who made me giggle and my mother who just put things in place. With all of this sunshine how could a small child of five see the dark storm clouds moving towards her two-story house threatening to rain on her parade? But the storms came and it didn't matter whether I could see them or not. I was made aware of their arrival with the announcement of my mother's sudden death.

One night I had a dream of my mother. She came in the form of a cartoon figure that showed only her face. She said she was leaving. She could not take me with her and she was not coming back and she loved me. I remember her being sick but I was too young to know and the adults were too old fashioned to explain her condition. Perhaps she understood that and the dream was a mother's attempt to ease the shock when one of her sister's decided to tell me, your mother died last night.

In my five years on earth, I could never remember hearing the word died used in a sentence, until it was used to describe my mother's condition. It seemed that I held my breath through the funeral and the relocation for someone to come and tell me it was not true. Of course that never happened. Instead, my three brothers and I, who tricked me at the movies, were distributed throughout a southern town like small animals who had recently been weaned. The boys were sent with a grandmother and I went with an aunt right down the street from them. Before I could secure the memory of my new home address, homeroom, and names of responsible relatives the aunt was kidnapped and murdered.

It was now July, one full year and several months since my mother's death. The body of Aunt Henrietta, who was violently murdered, would be found in the muddy waters of the Cape Fear River by fishermen. Her death served as my traveling notice and before summer's end I would be moved to the very town where her body drifted to. The death was classified as racially motivated. The FBI claimed they investigated her murder, perhaps they did. I do remember their dark suits and clean-shaven faces and the silence that would fall over the area each time their cars rolled in the yard. The final day of their arrival it was as if the earth stood still. We were five or six little cousins playing out in my grandmother's yard. We stopped playing to watch the dust rise up as the two black cars slowly drove down the unpaved stretch that lead to the house. The cars were parked close to each other as four very well-dressed men left their cars. They acknowledged us with a gesture of their hats and continued on towards the steps. We were too far back to see who had greeted them at the door. But we had become familiar with the scene within the last several weeks. Magazine reporters arrived, local police and the FBI were constant fixtures in the driveway. Each group kicked up more dust coming down that unpaved stretched than was kicked up to find her killer. It seemed like an eternity after the men entered the house as all events stopped upon their arrival. We were quiet and it seemed that even the wildlife around us in their silence waited for an answer. Then it happened. There was a hurtful wale that started low and reached a peak as it turned into a scream. It was Mama, my grandmother's voice that sounded like a wounded animal that had realized they had been shot and was resigning to their death. The news had been delivered. It was 1957 in the American South; Aunt Henrietta's name would fall upon a list of African Americans murdered at the hands of whites that would never be prosecuted. It would not be too long after her death that decisions had to be made about the children in her keep. There was me and her daughter who was around age fifteen. Although my brothers lived with my grandmother just down the street Aunt Henrietta shared the responsibility of their upkeep also.

At some point my adult relatives probably had another round table discussion to determine who would take the poor kids, that I was a part of. My younger brother and I were taken even further south while the older two brothers stayed with the grandmother. Before the summer ended a big dark car pulled up into the driveway without anyone ever giving us a hint of our oncoming departure. Off we went, back up the road a piece (roughly three hundred miles north) to what would become my childhood resting place.

Sis Rena, as she was referred to by her family was fifty-seven years old and I was seven when we became a pair. She was probably the shortest person anyone could ever be without being considered a midget. Her hair was a mixture of gray, corn silk like texture that hung almost to her waist. Although her hair was an object of beauty to me whether it was out, in the bun or in two braids piled on top of her head, it was as much her curse as an object of beauty. Her Irish father and extremely dark African American mother created a pale skin child whose complexion and hair texture served more as a sentence to her life than protection over her body. A fifty-seven year walk on this earth started in 1901 upon delivery from the daughter of a freed slave and sentenced to walk through life in the streets of a segregated American South until death arrived to take her back. Her journey had taken her to many ugly places but few she rarely talked about. When she did you could see the sadness in her eyes of someone who had routinely obeyed signs that read "for Colored only," attended funerals for lynched victims, searched the questions for justice and eventually became the relative of a victim who had been savagely raped, tortured and murdered, without a hint of vindication.

Sis Rena was a brilliant woman, whom I always felt lived in the wrong century. She was a female and was commonly referred to as a half breed. Even though her gender and race restricted her achievements in the south, she still managed to complete nursing school and become supervisor over white nurses in a time when that was unheard of. If she had left the country or just the south, with her brains and determination, she could have achieved many of her goals, even the ones that were forcibly filed away. Instinctively, she was loyal to her mother, sisters, and brothers. She felt her mother needed her help and she would not leave.

Many of her neighbors also benefited from her decision not to leave. Throughout our union, I witnessed countless neighbors seeking her counsel to address many injustices, such as forced sterilization on black women receiving welfare benefits (attempted by the Welfare Department). Another instance was when she got wind of me being taught something in school she did not approve, she was found at school with her apron because it had to be stopped.

When in my teens, she asked if I had planned to march in any of the protest marches held in our downtown area. As a reminder, my teens fell in the very heart of desegregation sit-ins, church bombings and other evils. I felt ashamed because not for one second had I ever entertained the idea of making myself available for police to put their scary looking German Sheppard dogs on, nor hose me down as if I were the fire out of control. However in years to come, my personal convictions rose up to meet the level of injustice I believed existed in my environment, and I am certain that Sis Rena was the source of my courage.

In her own way, she was tough as nails but kept a place for reserved non-physical affection. In our house we had three bedrooms and I had access to two of them after my brother left. As boredom or the full moon would overtake me, I would switch from room to room, usually every two or three months. When she went to the store, I would take that opportunity to rearrange her room as well. She never complained about those things other than the usual warning, "don't knock your ovaries out of place moving heavy furniture around." I could touch anything or rearrange anything at any time in that house, but never could I touch her. If I put my head on her lap while we were sitting on the couch, she would tell me to go lay down in one of my rooms. After the second or third time I stopped. In the first seven years I lived with her, we grew close in a type of psychic manner. We were able to do so because we never touched. Sometimes our psychic connection was spot on and others, I missed the mark.

Before global warming, when April showers actually brought May flowers and farmers could tend their farms based on an almost perfect weather forecast, this day a true April shower fell on me. My walk to St. Ann Catholic School was almost on its last leg as I had just crossed over the railroad track. I lied about crossing the tracks every time I was asked, even though I promised I would never do it. While I was just seven or eight, I was certainly old enough to see a train and know whether it was safe to cross some tracks or not. The alternative route added an additional twenty minutes to my morning route and I had to get to school well before the bell rang. I had to play, talk to friends, or finish the homework I didn't do the night before. So I was already a little distance from the tracks as the clouds turned black and in seconds crashing rains poured on me. School was too far to run to and I didn't see any houses in sight for me to take cover. In retrospect, I could have done that. I could knock on a door and someone would have let me in while the storm passed. Years ago that would have been a safe bet. Unfortunately that time and that safety has faded into the sunsets of yesterday. After fifteen or twenty minutes the pouring rain stopped and there I stood looking like a drenched rat. I was wet, cold, and confused. School was too far to continue the journey. I was soaked, and that would be my predicament for the rest of the day. If I'd returned home, I feared getting in trouble with my aunt and the nuns, so I just stood there and cried. Between tears I noticed a dark blue 1957 Ford driving down the street. My heart was filled with fear again. If I was standing that close to the track, Aunt Sis Rena was going to know I crossed the tracks and didn't take the original route. I held my breath as she got out of the car and headed towards me. She started with, she knew I got caught in the rain and she left work to get me. She had towels in the car and took me home so I could regroup. She never did ask me about the railroad tracks and I was so happy. I had been rescued, dried, removed and delivered to school where she would tell the nuns why I was late. Our psyche danced in a melody that day but several years later I would miss the beat completely.

She placed me in a home for a few days because she had to have an operation. I was devastated because for seven years, I had not been relocated. This was the first time we had been separated since I had come to live with her and I was breathless. I held my breath a little, waiting for it to happen. I relaxed a little more each spring when I was promoted and she would talk of next year. I thought to myself as I stood on the porch watching her walk to the car. What would happen if she didn't come back? Before she got to the car she turned around and came back to the porch and said, "Aren't you going to hug me bye?" My eyes widened with shock and embarrassment because I hadn't thought of it first. But why would I? In seven years I could not remember anything more physical than holding hands crossing the street, and that hadn't happened in an exceptionally long time. Where did this good-bye hug come from? I walked down the steps and met her halfway. We embraced and she kissed me on the cheek. I knew for certain then she was going to die and wished we had skipped the kiss. She didn't die. She lived a long time after that and surprised me again with another act of spoken emotions.

I remembered participating in a piano recital that required me to wear a formal dress. This was a moment to really strut my stuff. We were a scared group of about twenty young children who gave their year-end recital in the auditorium of a well-known university in our town. It was a big event that we had practiced for more than six months and finally the night had arrived. It was my first recital and certainly my first walk across a college auditorium stage. "Head up, pace your steps to the middle of the stage turn and bow," were our final instructions. "Don't be nervous just have a good time." That sounded easy enough until I walked out on stage and the auditorium was filled with people then stage fright gripped me. I bowed so low my best friend Marie, who sat in the audience with my aunt, said I looked like I was going to fall over. Then I sat down and couldn't find middle C for what seemed like forever then I began to play. Marie reported that I played one section three times that should have only been played twice. Once I did get started I just kept going and going. I was so nervous I forgot to count otherwise it was good. Marie also reported that my aunt cried during my performance and said, "I wish her mother could see her now."

The piano recital was the end result of many lessons introduced to me by my aunt, to include the lesson in willpower. My first piano lesson began in the summer months with temperatures between 85 and 103. Other than lunch or dinner there was no reason I could find to be inside the house once I woke up and finished what I had to do inside. So when piano lesson time arrived just in the middle of my discovery time outside it didn't sit well with me at all. First when she called I acted like I didn't hear her. She came and got me. Then once I was inside I moaned and groaned and did everything to get on her nerves. Quickly she reached her end and said if I didn't want to practice that I could go to my room. So the smart little girl that I was I opted to go to my room, I won. The hour passed and I asked to come out so I could continue playing. Request denied. I was not assigned to my room for the hour. I was assigned to my room on a hot wonderful summer day, still with bugs to find, cats to chase, and fruit trees to climb, until the next morning. The next day when she called me to practice I heard her on the first call and the practice hour found me at the piano in a complete state of comprehension. Without beating, yelling, and screaming, she had won.

My aunt took pride in the end result of her teachings without boasting. This was apparent when she commented "if her mother could see her now". When I joined clubs or excelled in typing her joy did not appear to derive from her ego. It was more as if she was keeping a secret promise to my mother to do her best by me. My progress was a reward for her efforts and would have been verification to my mother if she really could have seen me.

The day Aunt Sis Rena picked us up to go live with her we were strangers who happened to be blood relatives. In the total eleven years I lived with her, we would grow from strangers to family, I respected her honesty, her faith, and her relationship with God. The only matter that I knew she routinely lied about was her height. When asked how tall she was she would always stretch her four feet seven- and one half inches into a full four feet nine inches. I also grew to love her in the absence of the physical affection that she was unable to give. I would find affection in my grandmother's hands who would live with us before passing on to her final resting place. And I had all of God's creations around me, full moons, bright stars, sights and sounds that comforted my soul where I filed my hurts and all desires for affection.

My aunt did not take us immediately after Mother died probably because she was depressed herself. In her defense, I'm not certain if I would have wanted a seven-year-old child and I was fifty-seven. Within a span of three years she had buried my mother who died abruptly, a sister who was found in the Cape Fear River, and a husband who had taken too much of her in his passing. She had a lot of cats which provided affection. The cats don't necessarily require reciprocation, and they were low maintenance creatures. They played quietly with each other, they could be fed and left to come and go with no fuss. Young children on the other hand would require PTA Meetings, piano lessons, high maintenance, and the God-awful teenage years. It was probably the teen years that tested her normal sense of loyalty and influenced her first decision. However, after the second death and the possibility of more relocation for my brother and me, she committed to the responsibility of our upbringing. In spite of our ages, she committed to the responsibility to provide a place to live and give us the best life she could. To any comparison she did just that. We were poor, and that was a surprise to me, but we were loved and cared for. The benefit of such an upbringing is worth more than eleven years' worth of gold.

By local and national standards we would have been classified as poor. However, I learned from my childhood that many terms in life are relative and it would serve our sanity well not to get caught up in them. My environment was rich because it supplied all the elements I yearned to heal from a traumatic beginning. I was not the material girl and I was certainly not living in a material world. Moreover, as a child I was so inclined to miss the obvious or make the connection that we were poor and that it should matter. One of the best examples of this was a fifth-grade assignment I had to describe the color of my house. By fifth grade I had lived in this house roughly three hundred and sixty-five-days times a little more than three years. I knew the house wasn't painted but I never associated it to poverty, it just wasn't painted. My eyes found beauty in the nature that surrounded the house. And the house itself provided a safe place for me so I had painted it safe. After much thought for this assignment, I described my house as brown. It was a safe, warm, unpainted brown house that kept me safe. There were other things like no running water and a coal-burning stove that would have been used to classify our poverty as well. But there were other things such as a garden of fresh vegetables and five or six different types of fresh foods from April to November that raised that definition. Pecans grew wild, meats were reasonable enough to buy and all provided our bodies with the daily requirements of minerals and vitamins. Even our water that came from a pump came from a stream that was far less polluted than bottled water has become.

Poor or not I was the broken seed who had been assigned

to my aunt's garden for repair and in the process we were able to repair one another. Perhaps it was my lack of life experience that allowed me to regard life from a more innocent prospective one that had happy endings. I could not have known then but learned later that my aunt needed a breeze of innocence to push her out of one of her wilderness places.

Everything Aunt Sis-Rena taught me were principals she not only believed in but felt were vital to my spiritual and physical existence. I respected her for this more and more with each passing day. Often I would sit and watch her sleep and wonder, could my mother have done a better job? Only God could answer that. But I know that my aunt carried out the details of my upbringing as if she would have to give an account to someone in greater authority. What a world it would be if all mothers acted like that. Without a doubt she created a safe place where she taught life's lessons to me in her strait-laced fashion. Her approach to life was direct almost to a fault but it was a quality that I grew to appreciate. It saved time and established a realistic confidence because you always knew where you stood. She rarely complained and always believed that every problem had a solution, keep looking. Even her approach to segregation, which was the foundation of our daily lives, was not dealt with from a pity perspective, it was a fact of life that had to be dealt with.

It was strongly implied that the first aunt I had been assigned to after my mother's death was murdered by the KKK. Whether that was fact or fiction her life ended in a brutal fashion and no doubt instilled fear in the hearts of many. Yet there was no fear but more importantly no hatred in Aunt Sis Rena's teachings. God was always her source and this served to quiet her tone and motivated her to choose her words wisely. She was ever mindful that my mind was absorbent and was concerned of my outcome. Still her philosophy was simple don't run, don't hide nor live in fear just deal with life where you find it. Be kind and respectful to people and believe that you deserved that same respect. Speak softly, carry a big stick, and pray. To the best of my knowledge I think her big stick was God (and she slept with a 45 under her pillow) that and prayer always seemed to work for her.

Prayer taught me a stiff lesson in my developing years as I applied it to greed and selfishness. I was taught that God answers prayers and praying changes things. To a little girl of seven I was more than willing to put that principal to test. It was Christmas and the one and only thing that I wanted was a bike, red if it could be found. So I prayed. I prayed that Santa would deliver that bike to my house without the chimney in the poor Black neighborhood, with the outhouse and the water pump. I didn't care how Santa got there, he just had to come. A fresh cake had been baked for Santa with ice cold milk and I had all my prayers in place. All he had to do was deliver the bike.

As years passed, I thought of that story from time to time; especially when attempting to hide my true feelings from God. My aunt knew I prayed for a bike but what she didn't know was I went to bed feeling a little bit ashamed. I prayed to get a brand new red bike instead of my friend across the street. So what do you think happened? My neighbor and friend got the bike and it was red, it would take me another twenty years before I would have one to call my own. I had it for about three weeks, loaned it to my brother who ran into a taxi going down a steep hill in Manhattan. I don't think I've had a bike since. As life would have it, I learned how to ride a bike on the beautiful red bike that Santa delivered to my friend the neighbor. There was a great piece of my conscious that was relieved when I woke up to the bike arrangement. Aside from me and God, no one else knew what I had prayed for, but by the morning, I felt so ashamed and felt the need to take back the prayer request. But as it turned out, that happened anyway. Christmas would soon pass and each year would add more opportunities for lessons. Years were filled with the usual, don't lie, cheat or steal. Stand up straight, speak clearly and only fear God. But there was one area that Aunt Sis Rena was weak in. She never admitted her almost failing grade in forgiveness. I reached that conclusion through a specific subject matter.

When I was old enough to understand life a little better, my aunt revealed a piece of her life's story to me. She had visions of establishing a financial future and began buying up property to accomplish this goal. By this time, she married her minister husband whose health continued to decline until he was unable to work consistently. Consequently, she nursed him, and provided for many of his family members, who routinely insulted her color and degraded her profession as a nurse. It was enough to hear half-breed from outsiders but she had hoped for more from in-laws. In time she had secured five hundred acres of property. His help was needed to register the properties and she trusted him to complete that task. At this point, many may ask why she didn't register the property herself. Well, for the very young once upon a time when women only had the right to breathe, they could not register property, vote, own land, open a bank account that did not have her husband, father, or some man's name on. So she had to do what women had to do and that was trust that their husband would do the right thing and apparently he didn't.

As it turned out, he did not register all the property jointly much of the property was in his name only. By the time this was discovered his health was severely failing and he died before this action could be reversed. To add further insult to her injuries, the property that she had worked and paid for was willed by him to his family. Much of her life's earnings were invested in this project and the loss of money and the act of betrayal left her devastated.

In general, she had mastered the art of forgiveness and displayed this gift in her everyday life. Life's constant rejections based on her race and gender required issuing forgiveness in lumps at a time. There were no safe places, nor any times off other than sleep. Even there, it can't be said with certainty that daily deeds did not trespass into that world also leaving her with no place to hide. I remembered her talks of color and how she had been treated. The tears would well in her eyes as if she had suffered a lot more than she would ever dare to share with me. These experiences made it clear she had mastered forgiveness. But I was also certain she had un-forgiveness in one particular case. She might have felt she had endured her max and didn't have to stretch herself any further.

Initially, my life was too new to have understood the depth of her losses both financial and emotional. No one had hurt me to the point that I could understand how something like that could suck the breath right out of your body. Could it be that difficult to just let it go? My advice to her on forgiveness was strictly academic, just let it go. It was based on Bible principals she taught me or had paid good money to be taught by the Catholic School. Either way it was from an authority much greater than my own. But it was not convincing.

I then grew up and set sails to find my own adventures. Life with its cruel subtlety, would knock me on both sides of the betrayal fence. After graduating from high school, I took my courage and one suitcase further north. Too soon my wilderness places would spring up from the fertile grounds of the type of deception I was not accustomed to in the south. A handshake was not an agreement to be honored, family values meant nothing and neighborhoods were a place where groups of people lived, but not to establish communities worthy of much honor. The city, New York and Washington, DC taught me things I did not know and tested all my southern upbringing. Often I failed at those life lessons but I never forgot them. When I returned home to care for Aunt Sis Rena, I arrived as a rape victim on the heels of an abusive marriage which concluded in divorce. Women's liberation was on an uphill climb that hadn't come any too soon but not soon enough to have helped her. I had been dipped in and subjected to the many levels of betrayal and was better prepared to entertain the conversation of her loss. Even then when I suggested forgiveness as a healing source it wasn't very convincing.

Forgiveness is not an easy act to perform but it is necessary to one's wellbeing. When applied properly, it works like magic with powers to seep within the pores of the soul and repair damaged arteries and veins that have been clogged up with hate for years. It sets you free so you can see again, hear again, and move about with a light heartedness. Something is gone that you were unconsciously holding on to and you experience a new growth like a plant that had been once covered over by a larger leaf. Forgiveness works when you let it work but I am not sure that my aunt had that capacity left. I believe she was unable to let it go because her husband was already dead and she could never be offered an apology nor was she able to offer forgiveness. This is a tough position to be in and it would require a lot of prayers of, take me back to a place when it didn't hurt. You also have to recognize that un-forgiveness gives such continued life to a subject that it robs you of wanting to feel better.

My final return home had provided me with many life lessons all of my own. There was truly little that Aunt Sis Rena had experienced that had escaped me. So our conversations could be on a more adult level and I could speak with greater authority. I had a lot more life lessons to simmer in the principals of her teaching and had time to bask in the benefits of this forgiveness. My advice was almost elementary, it was the same. Let it go. Let it go by offering forgiveness to the act even if you can't offer it to the person. Something about that act, it removes a burden from your soul. It clears up your spirit to entertain other things and perhaps things that could cloud your heart from joy.

I can't remember exactly what words triggered this topic in the last weeks of her life but I was much more seasoned in life by this time and conscious of her death. It was not my job to stand in judgment. However, I felt that I had an obligation as a young woman who had grown to love her to beg her to let it go. My hope was that she could close her eyes and die in a place more peace than she was able to find in life.

My advice took. A day or two later, she summoned the Funeral Director to our house where the three of us sat and reviewed the final instructions for her funeral. She always planned ahead, a quality I didn't perfect to that level. Two weeks later she died.

    Ingram Street turned out to be my enchanted forest where Aunt Sis Rena, my aunt, provided the right nutriments for my healing and development. Full moon skies filled with bright stars or a slight frost for winter mornings served as one of many backdrops for my every life crisis. I can't remember what the street was called before they named it after Aunt Sis Rena and in many ways it really didn't matter. My home, was the two-story brown house that was never painted, the house that sat on the land covered with fruit trees, fig bushes, grape vines, and more than enough bugs and frogs to keep a little girl entertained. Ingram Street, where Santa never delivered the red bike and the lesson learned from that and all the other lessons would save me in all my years to follow. I started out worn like a broken seed, but I would be planted in a garden filled with love. In time I blossomed into someone worth taking to market. Ingram Street was not a place of wilderness but it was a teaching ground of how to walk through and emerge to victories from such places. I concluded that the condition of the seed does not determine the outcome. It really is the ground in which it is planted that matters. For that, I thank Aunt Sis Rena for her time and her life lessons, even the one on forgiveness Thank you…may you rest in peace…

INNOCENCE LOST
Chapter Two

When I left home, I was a bright eyed always wondering about something young lady. I had just turned eighteen without a care or a fear of anything in the world. I returned to my birthplace, New York, to be with my brother and his wife and also to see what the wonder of New York was about. Several weeks after I settled in, I set out to visit an older brother who lived in another borough of New York. This was before any aids such as beepers, Map Quest, GPS, cell phones or any type of electronic assistance. My travels would literally be cold turkey on a cold winter's day. I wanted to understand the twenty-five different train selections that were alphabetically and numerically categorized and its mission to carry millions of passengers throughout the five boroughs (small cities), as well as Long Island. One of these stations required for my travel, was created specifically for the transfer of most of those twenty-five different selections. It was necessary to understand in advance how that worked. It probably would have helped me a lot if I had ever taken public transportation in my human being life before coming to New York. Then I might have understood the concept of transfer and that all trains don't travel in a direct line. Or, if I had known that Grand Central Station would be a crucial transfer point in my travels, I would have been ahead of the game. Knowledge is everything and a sufficient amount of it is required for the success of any project.

The only thing that I really had a sufficient amount of on this winter's day was complete instructions to my brother's apartment, even though I didn't know how to use it. I was dressed in a thin sleeveless dress with a thin sweater that covered my arms. On top of that was an extremely warm coat for early southern spring but it didn't stand up to the challenge for a real New York Winter. My legs were covered with tights as I started my journey with wannabe pat-n-leather shoes with a sole thinner than bad pizza crust. My outfit was losing the winter challenge against sidewalks filled with old snow that had accumulated more cold and was blowing about by a whipping wind.

The walk from the apartment was about twenty minutes as the cold from the ground and the river beat upon my front and my back. I thought once I got on the train platform I would warm a little but that would not be my truth. The Vernon Blvd Station at 21st that travels into Manhattan from Long Island City is position on the top of the two levels. In the spring it provides a welcome breeze as the train comes into the station. In the winter, the spot is extremely cold while waiting and becomes even more cold as the train arrives. Most passengers wait downstairs until they hear the approach and then run upstairs. I didn't understand this process at first but I soon caught on and that was one of my first New York experiences that served me well.

There was a time in New York before graffiti when trains were just old, clean and could not brag about a central heating system. Heat came from little vents that were strategically placed at almost every other seat and I had no problem finding one on this Sunday when there were ample seats in the train. I propped my feet against the vent until I feared my cheap shoes would melt. Finally after the second or third stop, I recognized feeling in my toes and warmth moved up my body from my feet until I was completely warm and comfortable. I sat basking in this warmth dreading the stop when I would have to get off and brace the cold in my spring attire on a cold New York winter's day.

The train pulled into Grand Central where the cold breezed up and down the stairs that led to an uptown train. As I followed the directions, I sat near a vent to warm off the chill brought on by the changing of trains. After ten or fifteen minutes or so, I reached the stop on my directions and I left the warm secure place of the heating vent. I braced myself to enter the streets as I heard the wind even before I went.

At the very moment I entered the street I was lost – but it took me about two hours to admit to it. My "I can do this" ritual included walks up and down the same streets two or three times. There were blocks that looked familiar and I asked people for directions that led me down streets I had already been over and stops in coffee shops to get warm to start all over again. By the end of the two hours I was very frustrated and very cold all over again. I didn't bring a lot of money with me so my coffee shop warmups were limited. Finally, I spotted several men in front of a building talking to each other. They didn't look much older than me so I decided to ask for the last time, directions and if that didn't work I would give up the good hunt of finding my brother and go home. If I could find my way, the trip would not have been in vain and I really wanted to see my brother.

The two men caught a glimpse of me as I crossed the street and had their straight faces in order by the time I approached them. I explained to them that I was lost and showed them the address I was looking for. They knocked around some mapping ideas back and forth between them and finally turned to me to give me the standard version of how to get to the address on the paper. Their version was more complicated than the discussion they had between them. Just as I decided to just give up and go home one of them offered to show me where it was. As I saw no harm in that, I agreed because I really wanted to see my brother.

The young man who looked closer to my age was the one who volunteered to take me to the address and set off to get his coat from upstairs. He had only taken a few steps when he turned back and suggested that I go with him to get his coat and I could warm up in the meantime. By this time, I was thoroughly cold – not just my two big toes cold – but through and through cold. So I took him up on his offer. The building was a public place with lots of people coming and going so I never gave thought to my safety. Not only that, but I had been raised in an environment that catered to the wellbeing of women and children so I gave no thought that this would be any different.

The young man continued small talk as we walked towards the elevator. As we stood there waiting for its arrival I looked at him more closely and as I did I thought that he looked like any college student from my hometown and I was put a little more at ease. He was fair with curly hair, impeccably dressed and spoke well as if he had had come from a middle- or upper-class family. His look and the associations I placed with his appearance placed me at ease as he continued his small talk.

I would think back to this moment a thousand times. If I had to seek out reasons to put me at ease - then certainly - I was either in danger or in a situation I should have reconsidered.

The elevator arrived and he stepped to the side to allow me in first. Small talk continued as we rode up the elevator on towards his room until we were inside. It was neat, I thought, for a young man's room. The bed was made and covered over with a brightly colored spread. Matching curtains covered over the single window and I wondered if it was a real window or would it open up to a solid wall. There was also a dark wood dresser with items placed on top. It was there that I rested my eyes on a pearl handle knife as he walked towards a back room to get his coat.

As he returned from the back, I was still standing in the same spot. By now I was more than warm and even if I were freezing, I felt I should get quickly on the other side of the door and I could figure out getting warm or finding my way later. I headed towards the door in front of him as he put one arm into his coat. But before I could get to the door he scooped up the pearl handle knife, caught me from behind and pressed the point against my neck ordering me to undress!

Undress! Never. I was nineteen years old and had never been naked in front of a man – even the man I was going to marry had never seen me naked although we had been intimate. Certainly, I knew once we were married that would happen. Although I was shy I didn't worry about it because I saw that as a very natural part of a life that I was about to enter into as a wife. And besides, he would have been my husband. This was not a husband and not even a boyfriend. He was really a stranger now who I had given an opportunity to hurt me by applying out-of-state values to a foreign occasion.

At first I did not respond. I had hoped that it might have been a joke, or he was just testing to see if I would comply with his order. I stood quiet hoping that I would see his hand reach from behind me and turn the doorknob to let me free. But that did not happen. Again, he ordered me to take off my clothes as he threw his coat down and began to unbutton his shirt. In a blink, it seemed he had his shirt off as I remained standing in the same spot fully dressed. Seeing that I was not responding he didn't bother to tell me again to get undressed he began to undress me. Even though I attempted to hold on to buttons to prevent him from opening them, I failed. He managed to remove his clothes as well as most of mine with the knife either pressed against my neck or very close to my neck with the threat of cutting me if he felt like it.

The bed, that seemed so neatly made when I first walked in the room, now seemed to be filled with worms as I laid on it pressed downward by the weight of a stranger He pressed his pearl handle knife against my throat and he pressed himself inside me. I was shy and maybe stupid for following him into his room but neither of those two justified rape. Yet, there I was.

I had only been with one man and he and I had planned to marry. We wrote to each other over one year and came to know and respect each other in a way that people could only hope for. So when the time came that our love was consummated in a more intimate manner I could say it was indeed everything a girl would hope her first time would be like. Even the physical pain associated with one's first time was diminished by other acts of kindness displayed by the man I had come to love over a period of time. It was planned, it was patience and it was love it was nothing like what happened to me in that room.

First he performed oral sex, satisfying himself. Then he climbed up and pressed himself inside me. As he pushed further and further inside me, I felt as if I would split into. He continued to push inward as I pressed my mind further and further away from the worm filled bed. I fixed my gaze neat hanging curtains and further away I was removed until there was some part of me that just wasn't there anymore.

The loud noises he made as he concluded his assault on me brought my mind back as my senses became aware of a change of orders in the room. The room was now filled with the smell of himself which was spilled all over my lower body. That smell was combined with his stench sweat. Finished and fatigued – he stood. He handed over a towel that laid somewhere near the bed and motioned towards the bathroom where I could wash-up! He did, I did not.

At some point my mind and body became one again. I did use the towel to clean myself before placing my clothes on although washing was not an option. He appeared in the room just as I had placed the last piece of clothing on and was putting on my coat. He too had a coat on, although I hadn't noticed when he picked it up to put it on. No matter, I would now head for the door and was certain that I would not be stopped this time. Not because I believed he was ready for me to go but because I knew something in me would not allow him to do that again. We walked together to the elevator and stood in silence waiting for it to come. Once inside he asked me if I still wanted him to show me where my brother lived. I did not.

Somehow I don't even know how I managed to find my way back to the train that led to the Grand Central Station where I would change for a Number 7 train. I couldn't feel anything now – it didn't matter if I sat in a seat that had heat at the bottom to warm my feet or not because I wasn't cold anymore. I was numb. The only thing I could feel was his semen that was deposited in me and flowing out of me. Although I was fully dressed and riding on the train far away from him, he had taken a clean innocence and secure feeling and left a dirty, worm-squirming feeling within me in its place. After what seemed like a small forever the Number 7 train pulled into my station. The conductor's voice was my first piece of comfort I had experienced since leaving the room.

It was early afternoon when I had started my journey to find my brother. Although it was very cold, there was a winter's sun that shined warmth that offered an extra excitement over the prospect of seeing my brother. But by the time I departed from the train, that bright sunshine had long since gone down – not only on my side of this universe but in my very soul. According to the signs that displayed the temperature it was barely above 10 degrees and the wind blew with greater severity. But I welcomed the icy cold because now it didn't make me feel cold it was the only thing that made me feel the slightly piece of clean as it blew against my face. Now it couldn't be cold enough. I desired to feel the cold of my two big toes, the cold on my face, on my fingers, on my legs: essentially all over me. The cold was the only thing that held my sanity in place and made me feel clean until I could place myself into my tub filled with chicken scolding hot water that would wash this all away. What was I going to do? Who was I going to tell? What would I tell them anyway that I went in his room? No. I wasn't going to tell anyone and I couldn't bring charges against him because I went into his room. This was a secret that would be mine's forever to keep.

It was extremely late when I arrived home and everyone was asleep. I was ever so grateful for that because I didn't want to talk. I didn't want to be seen. Alone, alone, alone I need to be alone. It was just compulsory for me to wash and wash and wash some more. I had to be alone to do this. A strange feeling I could not identify hovered over me. I felt I had picked up some invisible person that had the power to see me but I couldn't see him. No matter what I did, he would be just around the corner waiting to jump out and remind me of his existence and of this night. But I held hope the water would clean me and wash away and I would emerge my old self again.

The sound of running water filled my ears and for what seemed like the first time that night since I had been ordered to take my clothes off, I exhaled. I was fully connected with the sound of running water as the saving grace for my mind, body, and soul. All I needed to do was endure a few more minutes...the time it would take to get into the tub. I fought off the urge to throw-up as I smelled his stench and was immediately reminded of his damp hand that he had pressed against my shoulder while adjusting himself over me. The smell of semen mixed with his cologne laced the bathroom as

I took off my garments. I continued to fight the urge to throw-up.

I didn't want to touch or even identify the clothes as mine at this point, but when I removed the clothing I was wearing, I threw them into a garbage bag and tied two ends tightly together to keep everything confined in that bag. I put on my housecoat and walked to the incinerator that was directly next to the apartment and dropped it into the already burning fire. Down, down, down it would go and soon burst into the flames that I wished I could have burned the memories of this evening in. By the time they were thoroughly burnt, I placed myself down into the running water. I wanted the water to be "hot enough to scold chickens" an expression I often heard as a child and wished with all my heart I could have gone back to that place, at least for this night. The water covered all of my body completely. Once in the deep tub I slid down until it covered me all the way up to my chin. When it was completely full and I felt that I had my protective covering over me I cried.

If I could have breathed for long periods of time under the water, I would have allowed it to cover my entire face. Over and over I continued to fill the tub with hot water as I sat alone crying and crying. Several hours had passed until I concluded I couldn't stay in the tub any longer. But as I removed myself, I still felt like Humpty-Dumpty. The washed clean feeling I hoped for did arrive with my exit. No matter what, I would never be able to put all my pieces back together again. What was I going to do now?

Days turned into weeks. If nothing else in our lives ever happens, time always does. I had hoped that this miracle medicine called time would dull the memory of that night. In a way it did. It dulled my memory of what he looked like. It dulled the overwhelming charge I had placed against myself for going to his room. But it could not remove that feeling that had come to reside in the pit of my stomach. Something so precious had been forcefully taken from me and no matter what, I would never be able to get it back again. It was that feeling of loss, loss of innocence, loss of confidence for my judgment, just loss that continued to wear me down. Every morning within minutes after I would wake it would start. No matter how much I washed or how hot the water was I just couldn't feel clean.

Days could pass into months without me running into someone who wore the exact same cologne. Then it would happen. I would be on my way to a happy event and the fragrance of the cologne would wrap itself around me and I would sink further down to my holding cell of self-pity. There was no change in my voice or my appearance only my behavior, and that was only noticeable to me.

This feeling persisted as time passed, and I appeared to be leading a normal life. Eventually I met the man I would marry and with this union I felt I would live, if not happily ever after at least live; or so I thought. I was wrong. I couldn't live because I filed my heart and shame at the surface of my spirit and it could be called up; even unwilling by the fragrance of a stranger's cologne. You don't live if every relationship becomes a string of promiscuity because you got too good at dividing yourself into two people at the very sign of intimacy. The other person escaped somewhere else to avoid smells associated with sex. You cannot live as you ponder a usefulness of foreplay that has nothing to do with sex. In retrospect foreplay becomes a permission seeking ritual. One partner asserts himself and the other surrenders a bit. Each physical motion releases a bit of control in each move of foreplay. Finally, it is understood clearly that the question has been asked and the permission has been given. Rape robs you the opportunity to give permission as the question is totally disregarded in the process of attack. Not only is your body assaulted, but your psyche is also wounded. You are stripped of your ability to be in control and you are rendered powerless as someone has their way with you.

So I thought I could live, if not happily ever after at least live. Years later I would discover how wrong I was when I realized that marriage couldn't fix anything marriage had not broken. Life as a rape victim would be just another something gone wrong to pile up on top of burdens already too heavy to carry.

Rape Victim was a title that had assigned me a place to live in a dark and gloomy spot. It was a place with no walls. It had no clearly defined boundaries although it securely held me prisoner. More than thirty years would pass before I realized I had been living as a victim for all those years and didn't know how to get out. It was the case of true Forgiven by Mistake that I would be rescued from myself and placed on a path of real-life living. It came late but I am happy to report that it did come.

UNTIL DEATH DO WE PART
Chapter Three

I'm not one hundred percent sure where little girls got their desire to dress up on their pretend day in the wedding gown that leads them down an isle to their own Prince Charming. I am even more uncertain why little boys have a fascination with war heroes or cowboys and Indians. I am certain however, that few boys grow up to be men that actually desire to go off and fight in war and I am certain that little girls never think that the isle of wedding bliss would produce anything less than Prince Charming. But as reality is our constant companion, we will come to know that the prince is not always charming and war hero stories are often reported by those who can best suppress the whole truth. But truth that requires suppressing is like anything held down, it is always on its way up and it arrives like a summer storm. First it's the dark clouds. That was his memory. 'Clear the village, kill all; even women and children.' Then there is the lightning and thunder, they were his regrets. Military orders followed but could not erase the lifeless eyes from his memory – they were buried but his guilt was not. Finally he became a husband and his Vietnam memories spilled over into his world as nightmares and too soon became my living reality of violence. We both grew in the truth that Prince Charming could never be a soldier and a soldier could never be freed from his past. A sad state of affairs because he did what he was ordered to do but no commander had the gift to order him or any other soldier the freedom they desperately required.

It could be correct to say that the Marine Corps can turn and will turn boys into men. It would be even more correct to say that those boys who were turned to men from the Vietnam War were instructed to participate in the war as killing machines. Unfortunately, men are not machines; they are human. Those who survived their tour of duty stored their wartime memories inside a mind without an on/off switch and left me with the questions. How many women and children were on the receiving end of a soldier's tour of duty once their duty assignment became home? No one would ever know exactly, but I can say for sure there was at least one family who could answer that and it was mine.

Before a tour of duty there was a man who was young, single, and filled with hopes and aspirations all of his very own. Imagine, if you will, that you are a high school senior in 1964 and your basketball achievements have been recorded in local and national papers since high school. You've been offered scholarships to attend major schools to play ball and an NBA contract is but a piece of paper, some black ink, and a few years away. Girls are ringing your phone off the hook and everyone wants to be you or be around you. You're not obnoxious you're just gifted and happy to be young and the one with the gift. Your dreams are clear ball all the way. It's just a matter of which school it's going to happen in, and you are emphatic it's going to happen! Then all of a sudden it looks like you have the gambler's hand that could never lose, but you just did.

Vietnam was some foreign place far on the other side of the world that was making news while you were making high school basketball points. An invitation was extended, come help fight in foreign lands and kill some of its citizens for reasons that might still be unclear. You were drafted and you couldn't say no so you accepted. Your home away from home becomes a jungle with unfamiliar sights and sounds that would be better fitted to a horror movie. A once innocent young boy is about to become a man who found himself behind a menacing riffle that cut through bodies of the old and young. Orders of the Sgt. Search and Destroy Missions ordered up like after dinner coffee. Unfortunately, the transition from boyhood to manhood could not have been accomplished with the proper level of understanding. So each mission left him standing unable to blink not knowing where, nor how to put the hurt away. Months upon months upon more months the tour of duty stretched a path that lead to a different destination for each participant. Not too mortally wounded could be equated with living because it just meant not physically dead. How long could a whole person exist a combat duty where smiles from small children were torn away with the bomb they wore to kill you? Who is the enemy? Why is there an enemy? When will this Hell ever end?

My husband went to Vietnam in the late 60's when Americans were burning bras and sitting in for peace while Viet Cong and American soldiers were killing one another as if it had become a personal hobby. Like some Vietnam soldiers, my husband completed his tour of duty without complete loss of limb. By some standards he might have been referred to as fortunate. What was taken from him could not be measured by two legs that could fit into a pair of pants or how well he filled out a dress shirt. One of the two legs needed to resume a basketball career was damaged during this tour of duty and the mind that might have bridged the gap between war and civilian life was torn to shreds with the remorse of war deeds. Each dig of dirt, another set of dog tags collected, body bags and propaganda, he could still remember where along the way he had actually lost his mind.

Like many of the soldiers who toured in Vietnam he was young and innocent to the type of killing and dying that would become a wartime routine. I discovered many years after the fact, through our children, that he made a tape during a psychiatric interview at the Veterans Hospital where he described the type of killing that he was ordered to commit. This taped section was conducted many years after the war but his confessions came from wounded places still fresh enough to cause him to weep. How do you overcome the type of madness generated by this war that was too large to mentally embrace? You must, but how? You don't, and the uncontrollable outburst of violence is the verification that it can't be overcome. And so it would be the honorable discharged marine who became the abusive husband as he embraced drugs and alcohol addiction to silence the screams of his war experiences. He joined together in a not-so-holy matrimony to a rape victim who perfected withdrawal without obvious notice to an art form and complete science. Friends and family would be invited to participate in proving that ignorance could be bliss while mulling over scriptural meaning of "what God has joined together let no man put asunder."

When I married my husband, I was incredibly young and had no understanding that we both required counselors, certified and professional because we were certifiable. We looked-for counselors who were spiritual not religious and had the ability to recognize our pain and assist in identifying methods to work through our problems. Not offer up hell fire and damnation for thinking about divorce because that was the only level of assistance I could identify.

Together, we were a mess. I lived in a quiet state of shock from a rape that he never knew occurred. While he self-medicated himself enough in hopes of keeping sights and sounds at a safe distance. The war was never discussed in our house on good days. You would never know he was a veteran. On other days you could not forget. To revisit "what God has joined together" would have been a leap; yet that is what we attempted...to be joined together.

I had always thought about being married. Some little girls dream of that along with the white horse. I can never remember using up one minute of my time praying for the right husband and I certainly didn't spend any time praying to get over the rape. I simply lived from day to day. I went to work. Rarely did I go to church and when I did it made me feel better but it was not consistent enough to matter. For the most part my life continued in that manner.

Several years passed and we had two children, good jobs and were looking at a home on the outskirts of Maryland. From the outside in we were a prosperous young couple who lacked for nothing. Upon closer examination you might see the bruises on my body from the many fights we had. If you could see inside of me, you would know the fear I harbored for my husband or the trapped feeling that I endured daily. On quiet days one could hear a sound coming from my husband that was working its way into a scream and violence would soon follow. He was a good father and a brutal husband. I did not want to break up my home but how many beatings could I live through?

Even though he had a lot of issues regarding his war past he was a good father who bought shoes every three months, more than enough Christmas gifts and all the Easter bunnies a child's room could hold. What more could a wife want or need? Well, I wasn't an experienced wife because I had never been married before. However, I felt certain there were some things that were not supposed to take place. Like, getting beat-up several times a month, getting thrown off my bed with the mattress on top of me, enduring forced sex because he was my husband and entitled to whatever he wanted. No matter how I tried, it didn't appear that this normal family thing was going to happen. We both had good jobs and enjoyed the finer things that life could offer. We had a nice apartment and were looking to buy a home in Maryland and we had a combined income to be nearly debt free. He was extremely thoughtful of good credit and paid bills, rent and car notes on time. Good credit should never be underestimated. On the surface it appeared that we had the marriage to die for. Deeper inside someone was dying and it was both of us. The fighting had become so constant that I lived in mortal fear. Every day around five to five I would start with a headache because it was time to go home from work and I never knew what awaited me there. I was most relaxed when he said he had to work overtime or he would be gone for several days.

By then I had created a routine of my own. Every six months or so I would leave, but I would always return. He would come get us from wherever we had gone crying to plead his case of regret. Then one day someone said to me that I ought to stop. Either you go and stay with him or you leave and stay gone. I thought about that for a long time because it had merit somewhere in it. So I decided to stay with him for one full year. No matter what happened I would not leave. I had to know before God and my children that I had given this marriage my best shot. Well, you would have thought the very gates of Hell had swung open and all the extra demons Satan could spare for this assignment had settled in my house. The violence had become so consistent that I had set aside some quiet time to figure out how to kill him without going to jail. I would sit for hours in the middle of the bed rocking and thinking but I just couldn't come up with a story. I am not a liar or at least not good enough to get away with murder. I'm not a killer either but I had reached a place that I felt death was the only answer and I wasn't looking to kill myself. During the time I was rocking in my bed something more useful came to my mind, why don't you just leave? Leaving had never been the best option because I was raised in churches and school churches where divorce was never an acceptable practice. It seemed that murder would have been a more forgivable wrong than the stigma of divorce but murder was resting high on my agenda.

I had a close and trustworthy friend whose husband had a legal gun. We agreed that she would get the gun for me and the next time he began to beat me up I could defend myself. I didn't really want to wait until the next fight although I was certain that would only be a few days. In my mind I had already worked out a plan. I wanted to shoot him first just to knock him down. Then I wanted to shoot him in places where he would have a slow death and I would eat dinner, desert included while he died a slow pain filled death! It was just. His death should be no different than the life he had made for me. He should know the pain of a fractured jaw, loose teeth, black eyes, black and blue marks all over the body. He should know the fear of knowing that someone had the power over you and just what it was like to live in mortal fear, not from a foreign enemy but from a domestic wife. He should endure the humiliation that comes with the act of rape that a husband performs immediately after he beats you to reaffirm that he was the husband. His slow pain filled death, in my mind, it seemed just. Just what he deserved.

For two weeks I arranged these details in my head. My one year was almost up. I stayed. I wanted to know I had done my best to keep the marriage and in my mind I had. "Until death do we part". Whose death and by what means? I had died, he had killed me every time he opened his mouth to call me a bitch or announce my unworthiness in some other area. He killed me through omission each time he dressed like a GQ Model to go on a date with women he never admitted seeing. I died with each gift that grew in value, they became commensurate with each beating. Like a salary, the gifts represented my endurance. Depression eased taste from my mouth, brightness from my sight and robbed me of sleep that kept me from my resting place which could only be found in my dreams. In increments of incidents I died. He had killed me so thoroughly I only needed a coffin. 'Til death", it would be but it would be his death.

I have seen prison shows with female prisoners who were accused of killing their husbands because they were abusive. I would feel indescribable sorrow for those women who truly had killed in self-defense. It is difficult enough to explain to a jury, who has never set on a couch growing rapidly afraid with each passing second that would bring her abusive husband home. It's even more difficult to explain, how a person who used to hide frogs from her older brothers to keep them being used as frog-balls for their brother's evening amusement, could contemplate the murder of another human being. You have to know the fear that strikes in your heart when you hear the keys turn at the door and your heart pounds uncontrollably because you don't know what you might have forgotten to do that will send him off in an abusive rage. I watched these programs from time to time and know in my heart that anyone of those women could have been me if I decided to take the offer of the gun.

It was odd. I thought about it later. It was never the fear of Hell that kept me from plans to kill my husband. It was fear of confinement. My greater fear was prison although the thought of the church not approving my divorce gave me pause, brief though it was. The interpretation of "what God has joined together," is a tremendous burden to place on a young woman or young man who is suffering. I reached a state of my own forgiveness for making a wrong choice. I accepted that I had not conferred with God to make this union so why then would I hold myself responsible that God might have joined us together? Somewhere, sometime during the great plan for my husband's demise something pulled me back. Leave, leave him because that is an option. At last, reason showed up. That was the time that I took my marriage to God.

The combination of the rape and a marriage that came from the bowels of Hell had placed such a mark on my self-esteem that it would take a personal relationship with God to find my way out of the hole. Not only was I afraid of my husband, I had allowed him to whittle away at me with his verbal insults. "You ain't nothing, nobody's ever going to want you. You're stupid, fat, and ugly. I'm surprised that you lived this long being that stupid." Every word in the dictionary that could be used in a negative context eventually came from his mouth as he applied them to me. At some point I began to believe what he said was true. Our daily activity continued, we worked, picked up the kids from daycare, and began house hunting to move out of the apartment.

One Saturday morning, as I rested between the worlds of murder and divorce, we met up with a realtor on the outskirts of Maryland to look at a corner property. It was an absolutely beautiful house. It was that corner property that so many newlyweds include in their five to ten-year plan. The good news for us we would be completing that to-do-list item within less years than that. It was the four bedrooms, hardwood, (original that is) newly decorated kitchen with all modern appliances. There were glass sliding doors that led out to an exceptionally large backyard. That was the yard that often comes with the prized corner lots. It was amazing and so worth the GI Bill that enabled this Vietnam Veteran, his young wife and their two beautiful children ownership.

I watched my husband walk around as he talked with the realtor acting as if we really had a normal household. As we moved further into the house looking around at the kitchen, the many baths and finally the bedroom. It was in the bedroom that my marriage had come to a mental end. A new house would only mean a new house with the same old wife beating and raping habits. I stayed as long as I did because he was a good father to the children and I didn't want to break up my home. I did however realize one day our family would be broken and that would be when we used that "death do you part" clause of the marriage vows. He would kill me one day and the children would be without a mother. He might get a year and return as their father. I would kill him one day and get life and they would still be out of parents; or we would kill each other one fine day. None of those were good options. It was then that I took my marriage to God. I believed that I had tried all the options to remain the wife but my safety and freedom were both in question and were being held by an unqualified gatekeeper. Although I wanted the marriage to work, I felt the battle had been lost and any fight would have been without cause. In his defense, he had problems that required his forgiveness that were out of his control. Most of that information would not come up for more than twenty years later but I couldn't afford to wait because my condition was already critical.

By the time I packed up the children and left my husband, I was twenty-two years old. In a span of three years I had been forced to reside in a Wilderness Place as a rape victim. I lived every single day feeling as dirty as I did the night of the rape. I washed, and used perfumes but I still felt like someone spit on me and I would never be clean again. Being a wife could not change that, being a mother would not quiet that. I wanted to get past that but couldn't find the road that would lead me out so I just lived. Leaving my husband set me free of physical and mental abuse caused by the marriage. But as I packed our bags to leave, I also packed the dirty feeling of a rape victim and together we all moved to a new home. In time, in another season I would revisit these war wounds with the proper knowledge to lay them to rest. And this would be such good medicine as I had learned something else in my travels. Reality is our constant companion and what doesn't get fixed simply stays broken and lives on until it is laid to rest.

SEVENTY-TWO HOUR NOTICE
Chapter Four

I was raised in a home that was God based without the extremes so often associated with current day religion. Life's experiences did serve as my up close and personal teacher where I could develop a personal relationship with God on my own terms without having to meet a midterm level type approval from onlookers. Further down the road I would be asked if I had a personal relationship with God, and I would lie and say yes. But this question gave me reason to look back over my life and especially the upcoming situation and believe that it wasn't as close to a lie as I thought.

Always, I had acknowledged God but looking back it seems at that period of my life it was from a distance. There was no fire in my heart for my relationship with God and it could best be described as limp. The most consistent thing I did was say my grace before eating. But to say I had a personal relationship with God as my creator or friend whom I could talk with while walking through a park or see him in a setting sun, I clearly was not walking on that street in my life's journey. Perhaps because I was so happy, by comparison to my past, I thought my need for prayer was not so necessary. I didn't need to be delivered from anything, so saying grace at mealtimes and a prayer at bedtime, if I remembered, should have been enough.

My children and I had settled down to a daily routine of happiness because I had the man I loved. He gave my life a new kind of meaning. We were a young financially successful family with credit cards, stock options and a new baby on the way. Life was good and we were happy. Like most people in my circle, we dropped the kids off at the sitter, caught the train to work promising every day to get up sooner to get a seat on the train. Every night we picked up the kids and returned home. I helped them with their homework while my mate cooked dinner; after which the evening came and we fell gratefully into a semi-conscious state of sleep.

Though I grew close to God during the end of my troubled marriage, I was in a different relationship that was peaceful. Peace is quiet and lacks the urgency of assistance. But one day was slowing creeping around the bend and I would have another opportunity to call upon the Him called God.

Our new baby was due in December and by all accounts it looked as if he might be a Christmas baby. Aside from being two and a half times larger, I didn't suffer from any medical setbacks. Around my sixth month of pregnancy, I was allowed to arrive to work one hour late and leave one hour early to avoid the rush hour after fainting at the very top of the escalator of the Grand Central train station. I remember feeling faint close to the top of the escalator and praying, "Oh God, please don't let them hurt my baby." I did everything I could remember to keep from fainting. Pant like a dog, take deep breaths, hold your head down but nothing worked. Just as I reached the top when the step levels with the floor I started going down. I could hear some ladies screaming, "Oh my God, help her before she's trampled to death." "Trampled, oh no!" I went down feeling like a mouse under a thousand feet. Hands pulled me from several directions as everyone scrambled to get me up as people were coming off the escalator in mass production style. Through combined heroic efforts of old ladies and even some Wall Street types, I was miraculously pulled to safety.

Several weeks after this ordeal, I went into labor while I was at work. I did not know I was in labor I just thought I was in a lot of pain again from another kidney problem. The contractions were so far apart that I was able to catch public transportation home. Sometime over the weekend the pain worsened and I was admitted to the hospital from the emergency room. I was in labor approximately six hours and continued until my contractions were two minutes apart. Around this time labor stopped on its own and I was once again just a pregnant woman with three months left until delivery. It turned out that I had a kidney infection that just triggered everything. I remained in the hospital for about one week and was discharged. In a few more days I felt good enough to return to work which I did until the final hour of the baby shower three months later.

I had been home only a few days by the time the "real" labor began. Only it wasn't as real as I had hoped for. One of the doctors rather smartly remarked that this was what doctor's commonly refer to as false labor. Well I want you to know that I was actively seeking real labor because we had been to the hospital at least six times and I had been in labor for what seemed like just one hour short of forever. Each time I returned home I broke into tears again knowing I would have to wait some more before I would give birth.

Finally the moment was upon us but I decided to wait until the contractions were almost seconds apart before calling the ambulance again. Once I did, they arrived with several police officers who had the job of waking up the father to be.

My two previous deliveries lasted within the humane range of time the first one was twenty-five hours and the second child was delivered after one box of Ritz crackers, one block of sharp cheese and six hours of hard labor. How much pain can one endure before they just keel right over and die? Labor must be the sure test of that question. But as my grandmother said, "it is the worse pain you will ever know and the fastest you will ever forget." If that were not completely true every woman would give birth to only one child. Given my past history, I assumed that this delivery would not be much different. But time would prove me wrong. Around 72 hours of labor and many visits to the emergency room the rehearsals had finally developed into a full-scale dress play. It was time.

We arrived at the hospital in the ambulance after a short and almost fatal accident caused by the thin and black ice. Several hours passed and just as I was certain I would die of natural causes, it happened. Saturday morning as the light from the rising sun filled the delivery room I gave birth to my third child. He was placed on top of my stomach. Once I felt confident that he was fine I gave myself permission to take that long awaited sleep. The labor had been long and hard but I was certain in just a few days I would recover and be home in time for Christmas but I wanted a little nap to get started on my way to recovery.

My son was now two days old and naptime was over and my baby was making a room visit. I fed him then stood up to do something and began to feel extremely light-headed. Since I had fainted so many times in my life already, I was too familiar with the sickening feeling you get just before you hit the floor. With great concentration, I walked closer to the bed with my baby in my hands praying that I made it there before I fainted. It was like wading through water. It became increasingly difficult to raise each leg but I made it in time. I never straightened up from laying him on the bed as I headed straight for the floor. My next conscious thought was of me in a bed as the doctors were summoned before their evening rounds to examine me. They stood all around as white jackets filled the room, asking, probing, sticking, and exposing. Although I was a new mother and just a few days before, had been exposed to public viewing, I was no longer in labor and didn't want to be exposed to the world. When they started I was strong enough to be modest and pulled up the sheets to cover parts while they discussed this or that. But my strength was rapidly decaying and it was an effort even to lift up my arm to stretch for anything by the time all their tests were completed.

The doctors completed their blood tests, urine tests and let me see how much we can stick you tests and they were off. Eventually, the head doctor returned and explained that I had a urinary tract infection along with a type of blood poisoning that must have occurred during the time I was in labor. The thing I forgot to do or couldn't do was pass urine during my labor. Not to worry they had prescribed medication that would surely begin to regulate my irregular organs.

Several days went by to no avail as my condition worsened. After another examination I was transferred to another ward, a terminal ward. This ward was filled with patients who were terminally ill. The first or second night I slept in the bed of a patient who had gone to visit her family before she died. I did not realize that this would become the routine for many patients in this ward if they didn't die before they made it home for that last visit. They were kept in the hospital to basically be medicated until they died.

Almost two weeks had passed and I was still in this ward. I had not seen my baby since the day I almost fainted and he was still in the nursery. My doctor was leaving for a few days and I guess he felt that he should set things straight with each of his patients so he stopped by my room to give me the speech. I had been in the hospital since December 21st and had missed Christmas and New Year's with my family. According to the news the doctor had just delivered I would never spend another holiday with them again on this earth.

The doctor stated that I was terribly ill and I would be dead by Thursday. Because my kidney had become infected, I still could not pass urine, my fever was 104 degrees and my blood pressure was 60 over 40 and was dropping even as he spoke. I had been given medicine, ice baths, shots every three hours, but my condition only worsened. He explained with a clinical distance that my body would soon go into shock. I would fall into a coma and from there I would die. 72 hours was tops that he saw and that would be used up by Thursday if not sooner. Well, was that clear or what?

What happened? This was supposed to be a routine birth delivery. The process was simple, go into labor and test the level of personal endurance for pain. Just as you were certain you were going to die, out comes a bundle of joy. God and all his angels performed some miracle causing you to actually forget how much it hurt. After a few days you and your bundle of joy would go home and your greatest fear would be the upcoming teenage years of time yet to be.

That was the game plan as we picked out the Christmas tree and presents. Once the baby was born on the 21st, we were certain we could make it home in time for a group opening of the Christmas gifts we had purchased with those special credit cards. But Christmas had already passed and my conditioned continued to worsen. When I was in a stable conscious state, I was able to comprehend the seriousness of my condition. I soon resigned myself to being absent for Christmas and present for New Year's Eve. Several more days passed as I lay in my bed watching the snowfall not remembering day from night and slipping deeper into unconsciousness.

It was now nine or ten days since the birth of my child and the hope of a white Christmas had passed on with old acquaintances. It became more difficult to remember the days of the week or if my family had visited me or when exactly they were there. I could remember things I had done as a small child but I couldn't remember what had happened yesterday. It was the most painful set of current events I had the most crystal-clear memory of. I had ice baths, given by the nurses to reduce my fever along with a needle that was administered every few hours. There were so many pinpricks on both of my thighs it became more and more difficult to find an untouched spot.

Doctors, perhaps it is their sanity saving method that they do not attach their emotions to a terminal patient and for that effort my doctor deserved a gold star. Although my conscious seemed under attack for several days I was most lucid when he gave me the end time news. When the doctor told me I would be dead in three days and the sun was ending on this day, I was quite conscious. I clearly understood the "you won't live past Thursday" part of his sentence. There I was young, a good life, a good family, good credit with credit cards, stock options and I had been given a death sentence. I could not be dying. This was so unfair.

I had fifteen to twenty years of conscious church attendance to three of the most prominent churches in North America. The Methodist Church, the Baptist Church and the good old fashioned down-home Catholic Church upbringing were all about to be called upon for some kind of guidance on how to deal with this problem. This was now my opportunity to use some of that which I had learned from attending these fine churches. With all this back-up, the absolute best I could come up with on such short notice, when given my own three-day notice of termination, was to be as selfish and thoughtless as some of the members I had encountered. I questioned God. Yes, that is exactly what I did. Me, a mere nothing when compared to the wonders of God. Me, the someone who could not even pass urine on her own, or even have the strength to pull up a sheet or make herself well. I questioned God. Why me?

A fear I had never known before overtook me when I thought of my children and remembered how I felt when my aunt told me my own mother had died when I was five. I thought of my mother who had died when she was only 33 and I began to cry. My tears running down my face was the most warmth that I had experienced since I became ill. And they continued to flow freely as a strange woman entered the room and placed herself directly before me. She sat down uninvited as if she were a personal friend and asked me what was wrong. Even though I felt that she was extremely invasive I couldn't bring myself to tell her things like mind your business or "hey, I'm dying here could I get a little privacy to bask in my sorrows?" For one, I really didn't have the will power to summon up that much energy and there was something about her that made me want to respect her. So I answered. I explained to her that I had a newborn several weeks ago and things went all wrong from there. I was really sick and the medicine that I had put my faith in wasn't working. Instead of recovering, I was actually getting worse. The doctor told me that I would be dead by Thursday because they had done all they could do. I didn't have to remind her how little time that was since it was already Monday evening!

She didn't look too worried one way or another, she just listened. After hearing the entire story she looked at me and said, "You need to pray." I need to pray? No, that couldn't have been her answer. What part of that didn't she understand, I was dying, I was twenty-five years old and I was dying. Although I did say she looked as if I needed to give her some respect when she said, I ought to pray. I was still as rude as a dying person could be. I spoke with all my energy and said, "I already prayed." Even if looks can't kill, they can certainly make you feel ashamed. She looked at me as if she not only could see through me, but she looked as if she had heard my first prayer. I lay there shivering cold because I just couldn't get warm and she made me feel even more cold and exposed me naked to the public type of shame.

She dismissed my attempt at arrogance and tilted her head to the side and looked at me as if she really had heard the sentences of my first prayer and she repeated herself. "No, you really need to pray." Her soft spoken, heavy accented voice went all through me. It was as if it had been a warning and one I should take. Much of our interaction was information gathering and advice giving, but like a mother she had given me a warning. She also gave me hope, I could not remember her exact words, but I knew that the situation was going to turn out ok. Without further conversation she stood up. She left me to ponder her visit as she got up and walked out as quietly and unannounced as she had walked into my room. And so I did. I really prayed.

First, I asked God to forgive me for the first prayer that was filled with whining and selfish thoughts, then I got down to the business of praying. I didn't ask God to let me live. I told God that I would not be afraid to die and I would not ask him to let me live. I was willing to accept God's will without further ado and I concluded my prayer. It was no doubt the shortest most sincere prayer I had prayed to date. As I finished praying, I curled up as a small child and positioned my pillows with my free arm to fall asleep. I felt as if I were six months old and was resting in the arms of God. For the very first time in many days, I was warm and completely at peace. As I began to doze off I remember handing my belongings over to God one by one. First my new baby, then my other two children, then the father. Moreover, I handed myself over to God without any reservations or questions. I let go of every worry; and slowly there was more and more space between me, stock options, and good credit until I stood completely free before God. At last I was at peace and I fell asleep certain that I would die and at peace with that.

Several hours had passed when the regular nurse arrived to perform her daily routine of torture and probing only this time it was different. She picked up my arm to take my blood pressure and suddenly looked at me with a shocked expression on her face. Before she could speak she walked quickly out of the room to get another nurse. They spoke among themselves as they took blood pressure and temperature and when they finished they called in several other nurses. Finally they finished and they all left the room leaving one nurse behind. She informed me that she didn't know how it happened but my blood pressure was almost normal and my temperature had gone done significantly, therefore I would not be needing the ice bath. This had all happened between the last time she had checked on me which was the usual three or four hours. No ice bath. For that alone, I was willing to pray some more.

Thursday was now upon us and the tubes had been removed and I was passing urine on my own and walking to the bathroom to do it. I didn't need extra blankets because I was warm and my blood pressure was absolutely perfect and there was no trace of a temperature. The doctor finally returned a little after Thursday and he walked right pass my bed only to do a double take when he looked up and saw it was me. He walked over to my bed in disbelief and commented "I expected you to be dead by now, what happened?" I looked at him, smiled, and answered, "I prayed. I mean I really prayed."

From birth to age twenty-five I lived in various places up and down the East Coast. In these many places I had been taught of God and had stored Biblical versus, whether deliberately or not. Yet until that very experience I could not have identified any particular time in my life that I had committed myself or my soul to God. But I can recall the feeling I had on that day when I prayed and offered my breath back to God. Something left me. Something like fear that had weight to it left me. After I prayed I felt clean as if I were starting all over. I'm sure that was one reason I no longer worried if I'd lived or died, I was free no matter. As I was preparing to leave the hospital, I searched to find the nurse to thank her. I provided a detailed description of her to no avail. I was told that there was no one with her description that worked on any shift within the weeks I referred to.

In the way of extraordinary life and death experiences, my life was relatively quiet after that. It had returned to routine days with highs and lows quieting the miracle of that time. When using the bathroom became routine I thanked God quietly but without the urgency to call Him down. Days would become months with problems within the second marriage that eventually rendered it over. Briefly I would be a single parent of three children in New York. I would attempt to make ends meet with a robe not designed for that plan. Philip Morris was my place of employment and had provided me with the greatest source of peace with a solid and sizeable income. Much later in life that employment would track me down in the way of forgotten stock, but at the present time I was about to resign. I was not moving to greater pastures but I was moving to a promise to keep. Aunt Sis Rena was ill and I was going home.

When I was eleven or twelve my grandmother was brought to our house when she became ill. I watched my aunt care for her until she died and I felt that is how people should be cared for. I made a promise to God that I would take care of my aunt that same way when her time came, and time was calling me home. I didn't want to leave New York, nor Philip Morris but I knew all good things I had in life were directly attributed to my aunt. In time the job and the town would be there if I ever wanted to return, so I was leaving.

By this time, I was in my late twenties with life's count of three children, two husbands, one rape, and the recovery from a near death experience. I had matriculated in life's journey to the position of seasoned traveler. I learned a lot. I was not successful in any way I could be proud of yet, but I applauded myself. I was still on the path to a "someday place" and had not forsaken my plans to continue my excursion until I arrived there. One day I would stand on the platform of the Grand Central Station waiting for a train while remembering some bad days that brought me to the good days. Until then it was time to move on.

DEATH & TAXES
Chapter Five

I was home less than one year when Aunt Sis Rena concluded her earthly journey. Her death struck my spirit in a very different fashion than my mother's. Irene Ingram, AKA Aunt Sis Rena or Grandma Nina had been my heartbeat on my every developing level since the summer of my seventh year. I could not turn right nor left without her in my memories, my decisions or my travels. Her death marked my graduation. In the passing of the mentor the student was on her own and real life was not going to take a holiday. It was really time to be a grown-up.

Of the many daydreams we have as children where we arrange ourselves as the hero or the damsel in distress, we rarely use jail as the backdrop for those private thoughts. Yet it would be a place I would visit after my aunt's death and left me asking a profoundly serious question. Why, Lord, why? Everything I have, hoped to have, or will ever be is related to the unselfish love and caring of my aunt. Throughout her years, she was filled with lessons and advice and even in her death I had more lessons to learn. If it weren't lessons to learn about myself, it was some important observations that needed to help me find my life's purpose. He who feels it knows it, but surely an email would have worked just as well. But anyway.

When I was eleven years old my grandmother became ill and was brought back to live with us in my aunt's home. I have fond memories of my grandmother and Saturday nights as we sat and watched Gun Smoke and Perry Mason. I would cry to spend the night because I could sleep in her bed but her covers were so filled with liniment which took my breath. Nevertheless, that didn't matter. I was with my grandmother and life was good. When I begged her to comb my hair, and even in her mild protest due to the arthritic pain in her fingers, she did it anyway. On the days she was resistant because she was just not up to it, she would still make my laughter box spill over. Grandmother would tickle me so much that I had to move from between her legs to stop laughing. My grandmother was a blessing to my life at a very crucial time. She was very affectionate in an old, long fingered, grey haired grandmother way and it served me like medicine. My grandmother lived between the youngest and the oldest sisters until her health failed and she was brought to our house with the oldest sister for her final days.

I knew it was a burden on my aunt. She had a fulltime poorly paid job, the responsibility of her own care and mine, and now her mother, but she did her best. My grandmother was kept clean and fed often with her favorite meals and I was her entertainment. Some of the neighbors came to give respite for adult support when my aunt was unavailable. It did help some, but even I knew it was still difficult. My aunt's long hair hung around her waist. She never cut it, but stress was a rude payback for her good. Her hair came out in the front like it had been cut for a bang.

In silence, I watched my aunt conduct so many life's chores like work and finding money to pay my school tuition. I can remember her moving about making things happen. What I rarely experienced was muttering or complaining. I thought she'd be in her right to do so, but she was the oldest, the poorest and most responsible. She was the chosen delegate. I concluded that in her youth she might have made a similar promise like I made in my youth; especially since she was brutally practical. It would not have been a stretch for her to decide while she was young that when her mother grew old she would see her through until the end. She never mentioned it, so I don't know what her previous plans were, but I do know she did her best and never complained and I promised myself I would do the same for her when she grew old. My grandmother had the love of Aunt Sis Rena, Mother Ivory, her best friend who was also an old lady, Ms. Nellie Ruth Williams, and several others. Early one morning, just as the sun was rising, her soul passed as she drew her last breath in a bed; in a home with family who loved her. I was a year older and had watched that exchange for that year and promised God I would do the same for my aunt.

My aunt and I had an odd way of communicating, probably like people who are remarkably close. When she called me on the phone, the ring always sounded differently, which let me know it was her before I heard her voice. This particular morning, I woke up with her on my mind, so I called. She called my name as soon as she answered the phone. At that instant, she did something she'd never done before; she asked for help. She said she extremely ill and she wanted me to come home. I went to work that morning and prepared to leave one of my most favorite jobs I've ever had. We cried and had a party and in two weeks I was home.

It was barely six months after I returned home that my aunt died. The expenses that were once divided by two were now divided by one income. We lived in an out-of-the-way neighborhood in the south which still had more trees than houses and was incredibly quiet compared to other neighborhoods. It was a good place to strike up a conversation with God and to find some peace from the loudness of daily activities. Quiet or not, it was not a place to hide from the long arm of the law who soon reached out to me. Before my grieving process had ended, I was arrested and held in contempt of court for non-payment of inheritance taxes. I was aware that they were due but the notice fell down on my immediate to do list. When the notice first arrived I made a mental note to take care of it and placed it on top of the piano. Then our lights were cut off at which time I took the kids to my girlfriend's house until payday. In the process of rearranging life I forgot about the notice. They did not.

They, the police that is, came to the office and asked for me. They explained that I was being picked up for contempt of court for not responding to the Order To Show Cause regarding the inheritance taxes and then they apologized. With that they continued to apologize and continued that it was close to 5:00 and they would return to their car as I closed up the office. They would wait for me downstairs and when I finished just come downstairs and I did. They offered me a seat in the front or the back seat of the unmarked car without handcuffs so it would look like I was just getting a ride home. At that point, it didn't really matter. I was thinking, since we had all these choices, what about the one that included me not going to the police station at all.

I had never been to jail in my life. I had not even received a speeding ticket and there I sat in jail on a Friday thinking Lord there must be a lesson in here somewhere. The following morning the town was hit with one of the greatest rainstorms I had ever seen. I felt that it was just my tears as I woke up and realized this really wasn't a bad dream. Welcome home, you're in jail.

The attorney informed me that I was not really arrested I was held in contempt because I did not answer the order to show cause why the inheritance taxes had not been paid. I explained to him the situation of the lights and so forth. I assured him it was not arrogance it was poverty that inspired me to rearrange my priorities. He explained to me that it was election year and elected officials such as the Magistrate who ordered my arrest was pressed for them "to show cause that they were competent and their jobs were necessary." One of the police officers who took my personal belongings couldn't believe that I was held in contempt and went on to say that it had been about forty years since that had happened to anyone. All I could think of was what luck.

The attorney explained that there was no bail because I was held in contempt. My freedom rested with the man who had put me there and he was going away on vacation and he wasn't sure when the man would return. Without further ado I prayed. "Lord, it's ME." The attorney said he would call him again and explain that it was my state of poverty, not arrogance that prevented payment. He hope that it would work. I was thinking what kind of attorney I had who didn't have any more courage than a mealy mouthed, I hope that it would work.

I later learned that both men would be running against each other in an upcoming election. Unfortunately, my attorney was not high on the pole and if his opponent decided to use this opportunity, at my expense, to stick it to him he would. The rain continued to pour as I sat in the jail cell looking out the window thinking how did this all happen. My children were safe away for the weekend so I was left to ponder my own freedom. Jail was a very new experience for me and like so many things I would come to be exposed to in my life. I never saw it coming, certainly, not for paying inheritance taxes.

While waiting, I watched the interaction of the women in jail. Some seemed comfortable at it because they had been there before and had not ruled out the chance of a return performance. While one or two others were there for the first time and the shock of it all was still clearly on their faces. Shock came and went with degrees with me. When personal questions were asked like "does anyone need a pad?" It was at this time that more reality hit me as you accept that your every personal need would have to be asked for, weighed, and supplied by someone else. Along with open showers and toilets without doors, it was an eye-opening experience. But the most disturbing part for me was the closing of the doors that night that locked every person in their jail cell. I really, really prayed. "Oh God please."

I called a childhood friend when I used my one phone call opportunity. They arranged for the attorney who finally caught up with the Magistrate and secured my release while the rains still fell. I was charged $24.00 for the accommodations for food and housing and I was released.

I was none the worse for wear and had been personally introduced to the Criminal Justice System in a way that would become even more personal. I couldn't imagine what lesson I had to learn in going to jail, a picture would have provided some good affects. Did I really need to go to jail? Maybe the answer is yes. "He Who Feels It Knows It," a nice Reggae song I like which rings true. That little piece of incarceration would play an important role in time yet to come in my future.

When that time would arrive I would use my experiences and empathy to help others depart or avoid such places. So did I have to go to jail? Maybe so, you don't know what freedom really feels like until you don't have it.

OBEDIENCE IS BETTER THAN SACRIFICE
Chapter Six

I believe that on every occasion when we seek the presence of God, we are not as conscientiously prepared to assist fully in the prayer seeking process. We ask, we wait, and we expect an answer. The new age, I believe, greatly overuses the teachings on, ask and you will receive. It seems to impose a negative influence on the idea of participation. That thought dilutes the possibility of a sound relationship with God as we do not participate in the give and take part of the prayer process. I think that it also lends itself to the spoiled child syndrome where the true appreciation for the receipt of goods is never realized because there was no participation in the process. Sometimes however, that participation does not require any run, jump, or hop activities. On occasions the participation is as simple as obedience and everything else falls right into place.

When I was a little girl, one of my aunts told me a joke that concluded: even though people were not willing to participate in their prayer request, that didn't stop them from expecting an answer. She said, "A man wanted to win the lottery and he continued to ask God to let him win. Day after day he asked the same thing, without any results. One day like always, he presented the same request. Dear God please let me win the lottery. The usual silence fell upon him and rested there for moments. Then the silence was filled with a strong voice that roared from the sky. "Go buy a ticket!" Even though I was little when I heard that and we were not allowed to buy lottery tickets, it was still so ridiculous that it made me laugh out loud. How could he have missed the most important step? Sometimes it's easier than we think as I was about to discover.

The leaves of autumn fell as I sent children back to school, returned to work after a week off, and attempted to prepare my finances for winter. So you see winter did not, as it never did find me without notice. On occasion it found me without enough money. I was always employed and maneuvered paychecks but the space between paychecks meeting varied between emergencies. Each child had to wait their assigned payday for what they desired. Children can have a gracious approach to the life when exposed to the truth. Overall, I think we were happy and my children never realized how much we did not have. Maybe they did but they were kind not to mention it. I remember a comedian once talking about his mother putting things on lay-away. He said they stayed on lay-away so long they went out of style by the time she got them out. It was good that he could laugh. I laughed because it almost sounded like me. But my lay-away items didn't outlive their season. Generally, I would have to return to get the money for another bill and return the items. But we had our payday moments so my children wouldn't feel that they were deprived of everything. We always had a car, even though the car insurance and maintenance competed with the heating bill. Still, each payday we went, as a family out to a reasonably priced restaurant. We would eat and talk and act like any family, with or without their finances in order. These were memory making moments I felt were necessary. We would not always be standing with our backs against the wall, and a vision of hope needed to be established like breadcrumbs that would guide us all out of this place. Until then, winter had arrived and our backs were clearly pressed against the wall. A way would be made, I just didn't know how.

Old Man Winter was huffing and puffing and blowing down my door with an electric heating bill. Electric heat did not serve our house well. The heat may have been clean but the bill was a low-down dirty shame. It was more than the mortgage and car insurance combined. Although southern winters are not usually brutal when compared to some other regions, it still required the use of an on button. The weather wasn't always consistent and the heat was used in that fashion. Heat was electric, cooking was gas, water was free but the bills fell in between pay periods and competed with food, Catholic School tuition, gas for football practice, daily trips to work and my night college classes. Each bill was equally important but demand was far more than supply.

The bills came one by one and I placed them on the piano. No matter where they were placed they would be due until I could pay them and I would pray everything would stay on until that happened. I was simply tired and very alone. The only relative I could count on was my aunt and she was resting in a grave not far from the house. I was working five days a week but never making enough to even think about making ends meet. When the phone was cut off, I was almost grateful because the bill collectors would not call and I could decide when I wanted to go to the mailbox.

I didn't want to spend any more time at my friend's house although we were welcomed. I had a house and I wanted to be in it with my lights on. But I wouldn't have enough to pay all the expenses until after I got paid. So where was I going? I sat down on the couch and just started asking God where to go, how was I going to get my appliances back on so I could bring my children home? I thought of this friend and that friend and everything came up to a zero. Finally I remembered an advertisement I had seen on television for the 700 Club.

When you are so heavily weighed down with problems it is quite easy to let yourself go. You begin to look more and more like you feel, beat down. I was a single mother again; I wasn't looking for anyone and didn't give a hoot who even looked at me. It wasn't a workday and I was going to ask for money. I needed to look the part.

I gathered up my three children who looked as bad as I did and out the door we headed towards the car to the 700 Club. Just as I got to the door something came over me and told me I should fix myself up. As badly as we looked, that voice could have come from anywhere and it would have been true. At first, I shrugged it off, but the feeling was just too overwhelming to ignore. For some reason how we looked was going to be an important issue this day and it was important to be obedient to this call. Important or not I continued with my children outside towards the car. I locked the door to the house and began walking down the steps. But the feeling persisted until I reached the car and it would not be stilled. As I reached for the car door the feeling, the quiet voice came again. Like a wave of instructions, go back and change your clothes. I didn't hear it out loud, but I felt it clearly enough to frightened me. I was afraid that if I had touched the car door, an electric shock would have shot right through me. To avoid that, I returned up the steps and back into the house for change. I looked for clothes that would make us look like God loved us. I found a pair of pants and

Wilderness Places

blouse I bought from the flea market for about $5.00. They looked as rich as they did when the original owner paid for them. I fixed my children up so they didn't look like someone just left them on my doorstep. Hence, we headed out again to the 700 Club. Now my focus was more on my inner peace from obedient and I didn't feel so desperate, and we really did look a lot better. We got into the car and headed towards the 700 Club looking like somebody for real.

When we walked into the building they were starting a prayer circle and I joined in. The children went with other children to play. They concluded the prayer session by asking everyone if they had a personal relationship with God. The people gave such enthusiastic responses as if God was their new best friend. That left me feeling like the odd girl in the room. I wasn't familiar with that concept of God as my personal Savior nor was I certain how you could make that happen. Personal relationship with God, that answer was going to be a little tricky. I prayed to Him. Could that count for personal? After all, wasn't it God who had ordered me to change my clothes? Seems like the question was still lingering in the air when I lied and answered, "Yes, yes. I have a personal relationship with God. For some reason I felt personal was a lot better than I had been giving God and I felt guilty. I had a personal relationship with God when I had my near-death experience before I returned home. But I had not been faithful to follow-up on our relationship once I recovered. Though I was mindful of the experience and on rare occasions went so far as to mention it to people, there was still something lacking and I was certain my current relationship was anything but personal. When I lied, I felt God was going to jump out from somewhere any second and yell YOU LIAR! When that didn't happen, I made a mental note that I needed to work on that when this was over. A type of alarm went off within me generating a feeling of sadness. I was missing out on something delightful but I could still get it just for the wanting.

There were several different counselors who were assisting different clients with different issues. I spotted an older lady and I prayed, not to get her. She looked like she never had an *'I need'* problem in her entire seventy-five-year-old looking life and wouldn't understand I was really doing everything I could possibly do to help myself already. My ends were just not meeting. My children and I sat only for a few minutes before I was called and who else other than that lady called me to be interviewed.

She moved slow and spoke quietly as I followed her to her area. She motioned for me to sit and as I settled she asked me to tell her my problem. So I did. I explained that I was working and attending school. I worked every day but I just had more expenses than I had income. She listened quietly and then asked if I had at least one relative that could help me. I explained there was no one other than my children.

She continued her interview while explaining that the 700 Club could only help with one utility bill and she asked again if there was anyone who could help us. I assured her there was not and I would work with whatever I received until I received my pay.

At this time she paused and commented that she thought it was outstanding that I was attending school and trying to make a better life for my family. She continued talking giving me other compliments on how nice we looked and well kept my children were as she reached down and pulled out her purse and removed her checkbook from its compartment. Even though I was watching her I thought that she had basically dismissed my need and was writing out a check for one of her bills. She continued talking as she wrote out the check. She signed her name, tore the check out and handed it to me. She explained again that she was impressed that I was trying to make a better life for us and stated that the check was the difference of what I required. Apparently I had a look on my face like, how am I going to pay it back. That was when she said it was a gift I wouldn't have to pay it back. She continued saying that God does different things for different people. I fought back the tears generated by the kindness of a total stranger. I was glad that I was obedient to the 'you need to change your clothes' command. We originally headed out the door looking unloved and certainly not, well kept.

This experience also served as a reprimand to me for jumping to conclusions about what people can understand or who people really are. I learned from that experience and so many others that God aligns people to assist you. She may have had similar experiences to mine or maybe she was just moved to assist me. Either way, she was the one who observed the end result of my obedience, go back, and change your clothes because someone is waiting to participate in your miracle..

EMPLOYMENT WOES
Chapter Seven

More time passed and more fires were put out with promises of new fires all the time. I was still a single parent of three crazy little children. I was still in charge of the car note, mortgage, heating, and air conditioning and all the stray animals my son could round up. Bills did not take holidays and any thought of unemployment caused my heart to shutter. And yet, there I was unemployed. Funding for my position was not renewed and no one was certain when or if it would be. So I was relocated to that, in the meantime position, what do I do. Many positions I had held in the university were funded and it was a risky decision to accept them. Because they were annually funded they were more available than some others. Also the immediate income of that assignment was a better bet than many positions that were not going to free up or were already assigned to someone in a secret promise. No matter what the reasons, I was unemployed and wanted to resolve that problem, quickly. There was one position on campus in the Chancellor's Office that was opened and I was strongly recommended for it. I was interviewed and several days later offered the position. I was extremely excited because it was a position with great promise. I could continue my studies in the evening at the university and the salary was outstanding. Yet with all of this excitement, something occurred during the interview process which concerned me. The Chancellor had a friend who was a psychologist and he asked him to sit in during the interview.

I did not make any objections although I felt their intentions surely were not professional. It felt like they were college boys playing a prank and I was the object of that prank. Neither men said anything inappropriate, nothing sexual but the questions were more from a psychiatric point of view. I was asked a question and I'd provide the answer related to the position. Then the psychiatric friend would ask the doctor question, why did I say this instead of that. The process continued in that manner for the entire interview. Less than one hour the interview came to an end and I was certain I had failed the psychiatric scrutiny, but I was wrong.

The secretary congratulated me and provided me with a date and time to return to sign contracts and get a start date. There I had it. A new job, ten credits of college tuition paid and a particularly good income. Yeah, so I thought. On the day I returned, I was informed the employer changed his mind and wanted to continue interviewing. It was a hit in the stomach. The secretary could barely get the sentence out of her mouth. For a moment I'm certain I lost my breath. Quickly I regrouped. I would have to process that information in the privacy of my own disappointment, inside my car. Once I arrived there. I cried. My thoughts got a promotion from worry to extreme worry. The mortgage was more urgently late than when I thought I had employment as a negotiation chip. What was there to do now? Look for another job? Look for other employment was the most and only logical outlet I had, but that represented more time. That would be more money out of the piggy bank that would not get replaced soon and without promise. So, I wiped my tears enough to see my way home and any tears left would find their way down my cheek until I pulled into my driveway. I couldn't let my children see that. I was going to work with what I had until. Even though the mortgage was due we hadn't been put out yet. One door closed another would open.

In time, I would learn that this man was fired for using the position to lure college students in with a promise of employment. I was in my late twenties and maybe not his type and the employment offer was just a ploy to cover up his real intentions. Often I wondered if they were the tag team and the second party interviewer was to determine who would be the best pick for their activities. But anyway, I was too consumed with the employment search to spend too much time on that.

Continuous searches opened up another opportunity with an even greater promise of learning and school. This position was in a very prestigious law firm. I had two extensive interviews each lasting more than one hour. How much information does a company need where three hours of interviewing would be necessary and only paying a dollar more than minimum wage? The first interview was extremely promising. The interview was with a partner who recommended me for the position. However, I had to meet with the actual head attorney who would make the final decision, but I was assured that would not be a problem. The day finally came.

The office was located in an office building that housed several law firms. It was a new construction and consisted of many amenities. The landscape was pristine. To the side of the building was a three-season mixed garden. From spring through fall several wrought-iron seats provided an advantage point for employees to sit and enjoy the colors. The colors of red, yellow, and green were a nice contrast to the building and the scene stood out when compared to some older nearby buildings. The building, although part of the industrial park group, was extremely inviting. Less than a week had passed by the time I had been invited to interview and I arrived with great hope and renewed self-esteem. The first lawyer was extremely gracious with his complements and after that last ordeal, they were greatly welcomed.

The office had a waiting room filled with large well-kept plants that accompanied the office furniture surrounding a well-arranged setting. I sat with confidence and preparation. I did my homework and was familiar with the type of law that was practiced. I knew the number of employees, their winning track record even the number of clients they represented yearly. As much information as I could retrieve I did. This was also the days before the internet, Google, and Wikipedia. Imagine if you can, that there was such a time. Reading and library research was not only fundamental it was mandatory to answer questions. My confidence didn't convince me that I would get the job offer. I wanted to be remembered as knowing something even if I didn't get the job. So finally, the office door opened and the lead attorney walked out, introduced himself and ushered me into his office. His office was impressive and smelled like new books.

I walked into his office and noticed black and white pencil drawings of the Market House placed on the wall. For those of you who don't know, a Market House was a building where fruit, vegetables and slaves were sold. In many southern towns, a refurbished Market House still stands on Main Street. The Market House in many towns is located in the center of town and traffic circles around it. Driver's Ed students often have the task of driving around it to learn the appropriate right of way for such traffic patterns. I like black and white art and there was a part of me that was extremely impressed. But, the Market House that dated back to the 1800's, there was a slave somewhere on the canvas. Why?

When I saw these pictures I was a little concerned but the interview was about to start and I didn't need to go down the road of Black History right that minute. We talked for about ten minutes about the requirements for the position and the phone rang. At first I didn't think much of it. He was an attorney and maybe there was some emergency that couldn't be held off. However, the phone continued to ring as he interviewed me. He would excuse himself, take the call while watching me during his conversation. Our interview continued for more than an hour with consistent interruptions until the interview was concluded. Finally, it was over.

At the end of the interview, the attorney sat back comfortably in his big leather chair as if he had concluded a good meal. He pointed out that he was impressed by my resume and that I was one of the most qualified people out of the 18 people whose resume he had reviewed. He was also impressed by my poise during the deliberate telephone interruptions. He admitted that he had instructed the secretary to forward his calls because he wanted to see how I would act under pressure. At the conclusion of his great admissions, he thanked me for my time and informed me that he would not be able to hire me because I was Black. He continued that the nature of his practice was divorce and his clients often came in angry and hostile. If they had to deal with me that might make them even more angry. Anyway, as he put it, he I walked already had one Black employee. Well, that was certainly calling the kettle BLACK!

Not only was I Black, I was Black when I had the first interview with his partner. I was Black when I walked into his office that afternoon and sat down to interview for a job that he was certain he was never going to offer me. I was just as Black when I walked out after he admitted it was all a game. Only then I was Black and mad.

Employment is extremely competitive in life in general. When you are not hired for a position, no doubt, many human conditions influenced the decision. And in many cases in the entire world race, gender, religion, sexual preference, zip codes and all other factors account for final decisions. But in my entire life I have never sat face-to-face with an individual who had walls completely covered with the Market House pictures, tell me he couldn't hire me because I was Black and my interview was basically for his entertainment.

During the course of the interview, my down time while he was on the phone allowed me to observe the office more. On his desk rested a well carved letter opener that took my memory back to Perry Mason. I used to watch Perry Mason, a Law and Order equivalent and there was always a case where someone was stabbed to death with a letter opener. It did look a lot like a knife and many were just as sharp. I had revisited the letter opener but I wasn't thinking of Perry Mason. I had clear and unapologetic desires to hop over the desk and stab him a few times just as he said, I can't hire you because you're Black. But then I was reminded of the punishment for murder, the county jail was just a few blocks from his office. I had already been an overnight guest there for contempt of court. That was less than charming. I gritted my back teeth hard enough to give myself a headache. Then I vowed no matter what, he would not see me cry. I thanked him for his time. I shook his hand thinking "now you go home and tell your family I was a lady until the end, you bastard, and I left.

On the real, I am going to cry until I have an asthma attack and die on my own bed because I don't have medical insurance. However I wasn't going to allow that to happen until I got home. I almost lost it a few times while driving and reflecting on the black-balled words, "I can't hire you because…" Once home I cried and cried and cried off and on for the next several days. What was I doing wrong? Where did this get all mixed up? Once upon a time I was married with a husband. But somewhere down the road my relationship with my ex-husband could read like some of my overdue bills "you forgot, but we remembered." My ex-husband forgot but I remembered that even after divorce, there were children who had to eat and who deserved a good chance at life and had to have money to make these things happen. Then there was the house. I thought of the house and laughed. I was obligated to be in this town for a while because of the house. I was experiencing tremendous grief with the never ending problems associated with the house. Trust me, I was wearing God's ear out and working on that personal relationship. These routine check-ins or desperate screams for help marked the strengthening of my relationship with God. I laughed sometimes because after my aunt's death, it appeared she was still teaching me. That was her role in my life from the day I walked into her home until the day I buried her. Eventually, the crying stopped and like before, the reality of my life remained. I had responsibilities and I didn't have the luxury of time to wallow around in my sorrows to mourn my losses. I had to find a job.

The law firms, universities, and a few other institutions paid better salaries in the south. Since I had used up two of these I was reluctant to go down that street again. So I decided to try another area even though it was seventy-five miles away. I had a car and besides when I lived in New York City, a two-hour commute was almost the normal. I could drive one and 1/2 hours one way in the comfort of my own car as I brushed up on my country and western, rap and gospel music appreciation. With resume in hand I talked to God, He was the pilot and I was the co-pilot. I had planned to pass out my resumes like it was something somebody really wanted until somebody said yes. I sat down and planned out my strategy.

Because it was North Carolina not New York City, there were no security guards posted in the lobby area of the Research Triangle area. My plan began with praying or talking. God you know my circumstances. I still had a house, Catholic School tuition for two of my three children, a car note, car insurance, house insurance, food, clothing, and I had the very nerve to have pets on top of that. Again, there is always some good news in the mist of bad news. Our pets were truly "country" pets. The dog could eat table scraps, I just had to make sure we ate so there were some table scraps. And then there were the cats if push came to shove they could catch a bird. If not, they could share in on those table scraps. The pets were also very good for our mental health so I had to make sure we all ate. All of these things God was still aware of. So I talked it over with Him for a day or two. Which way do I go? When do I go?

The Research Triangle area appeared to be the most

appropriate approach because they were northern companies that had moved south. The companies were located in the Raleigh/Durham area of North Carolina which was about seventy-five miles from where I lived. Traditionally, they paid a little more with more northern work attitudes that I was accustomed to. Monday morning I was off. Fully clothed in my interview suit and feeling more than confident and determined that by Friday afternoon, I would have a job. Again, as a reminder this wasn't the year of the original flood, but it was many years before the word on-line was associated with any technical. There was no existing internet, texting, nor sentences that redirected you with the "everything is done on-line." I took full advantage of this opportunity for up close and personal office attendance.

There wasn't a lot of money for this day trip, so I spent my money wisely. I didn't know when my next official payday might happen. I had some food in the house and about twenty or thirty dollars of real money. I knew I would not be restaurant shopping, so I made sandwiches, packed juice, and some water and off I went. I accommodated my cigarette addiction with a supply to last a week or so. In the year of 1979 cigarettes could be purchased for a little more than fifty cents a pack. I was determined to keep as many unlit as I could. They weren't really expensive but they were not free.

I went from office to office, walking from air-conditioned buildings into the blazing hot mid-day sun. The routine repeated itself Monday and Tuesday which was check gas-range, ration out cigarettes, pack a lunch and off to the Research Triangle Area. By Wednesday afternoon, I was exhausted and a little worried that I might not have a job by Friday. I was running low on gas, cigarettes, and cash. I fought off fear trying to take a seat in my stomach. I prayed some more and returned on Thursday and stayed all day from 9 to 5 as I had to. Something had to give! Someone was going to hire me!

My resume had been circulated from one end of the Research Triangle to another. People probably talked about that crazy lady who went from office to office asking if she could leave her resume or did anyone need a secretary. Finally, my labor paid off. An architecture firm desired a person to type prospectus for one of their new projects. The former employee left abruptly for a better position and the company needed someone to start right away. The firm was extremely good to me. The owner was an older man whose religious practices had the office close early on Fridays. That was certainly a blessing for me because family time would last longer if I got home earlier. The company was having a cash flow problem and some paydays employees had to wait until Monday to receive their pay. That was never my issue. The secretary always gave me my check at noon on Friday and instructed me where to go to get it cashed. This was also a time before direct deposit.

The job was a blessing in many ways because, for one, it brought up my self-esteem, which was daunted by two rejections, I was serving by answering someone's problems, and it gave me value in a paycheck. I continued with the architecture firm until I secured employment closer to home. Arrangements were made to catch up on my mortgage. Eventually winter turned to spring and reduced my monthly bills by one.

I learned several important lessons from that trio of employment confusion. Securing employment requires a combination of things we are taught in school. The basics are education, training, experience, references, and a few other essentials. The other influential factor isn't talked about much in the classroom but needs to be. That element is the human factor. Relentless interviews, no call back, or the quiet and hurtful emails, a candidate has been chosen for the position can leave you stunned. Eventually, you feel luck of the draw would be required to get the, you're hired sentence. Once I worked in Human Resources I had firsthand observation opportunities of how the ugly employment game is played. I observed how personal influence can carry more weight than the truth of a good resume.

In-house positions have to be posted to pretend that favoritism is not at play. Fifty or sixty people may apply for the same position, depending on the market. Often a person has already been offered the position but the offer cannot be valid until all who apply are eliminated. That process typically arrives in an email that states, someone else was chosen. Then there are those occasions when no one is chosen up front and a pool of very qualified applicants numbering eighty or more apply. In this case seventy-nine will still be truthfully disappointed. Among those there will be many whose self-esteem will be wounded but they need to regroup and move on. Eventually one will be that one and the many others will have to regroup. There is a lot of pull and tuck in the employment process. While human beings are certainly used to deliver the good or the bad news, in the end God can still be relied upon. In my case as two men were plotting and setting up their schemes for their entertainment, another man was being prepared to assist me.

God is not just the final answer; He is the answer. He

rests in the answer long before the answer is known. Problems have solutions, but sometimes those solutions require more leg work such as faith than other problems. How much are we willing to participate in the problem-solving situations. This question might be asked of us more than we are willing to own up to. I've had wonderful jobs that fell upon me, while others didn't come to me without a fight. When my children were young, I sought employment to satisfy the financial requirements of my household. As the financial responsibilities eased up, I began to look more for wages and purpose.

The wisdom that came from employment woes is simple. Employment is necessary for the existence of our lives. However don't allow ANYONE to damage your self-esteem. "You're hired" decisions are made by people with either fragile or strong egos. They'll be someone who will want you because you qualify, or vice versa. The trick is not to give up and as you march on try to mix purpose with paydays. In time, you will get the "you're hired" letter and things will be alright.

PORCH FOOD
IN MEMORY OF MR. JENKINS
Chapter Eight

There is a southern saying; There's never a second education in the first kick of a mule. Porch Food is an excellent example of how answers to prayers have layered lessons and are often delivered by the least suspecting souls. So often when we pray, we include directions for the process, sit back and wait for the knock on the door. We don't say it out loud, but in our heart of hearts we see it working out just the way we imagined. We are always wrong, and this is a good thing. It's good because each prayer experience continues to reinforce our faith because the prayer is answered in some odd way and it redirects our attention to the true source. It is also a good opportunity to teach us how God aligns the necessary players for our benefit and uses that opportunity to assist the deliverer in some way also. Porch Food is probably one of the shortest stories I have to share with some of the most important lessons for good long-term living. It also gives me an opportunity to remember a Veteran, a good man and a man who helped me out of one of my many single parent crises.

Almost a month had passed since the beginning of my recent employment. This job had come by way of faith, fortitude and relentlessly knocking on door after door seeking employment. It was an architect firm that was experiencing some cash flow problems of their own. But the secretary always secured my check and the bank that would clear it so I was never one that experienced a paycheck cash problem. Little by little I caught up on back bills and was getting a little order to my finance. But like all good plans, then one day happens. One day, on this particular week it was about two or three days before payday and I was down to my last few dollars. It was a toss-up between buying gas to get to work to get paid or buying food. I had talked with God for most of the seventy-five-mile trip home. A few times I thought of the question the lady from the 700 Club had asked me when I had gone there for help. "Isn't there any one you can call on; you don't have any family here?" The answer was "no" then and it was still "no" on this day. That answer made me feel even more alone. There was no one. This statement barely settled in my heart as I thought, I may not have flesh and blood sitting in the passenger side, but I do have God. Sometimes I thought, it would be nice if I could see Him in the passenger seat. I almost laughed out loud at that thought of an appearance in my passenger seat. The privilege of feeling Him was going to remain the best option and I was going to allow those feelings to dictate my behavior in securing food for my family again.

Since the visit to the 700 Club where I was questioned and left filled with guilt about my lack of a personal relationship with God, I felt confident that this latest prayer demonstrated my surrender and I should get some high scores by now. Then maybe I was a little hard on myself. I confused church attendance with the personal relationship with God question, on that I was slacking. Again, in my defense I believed in God and had established that relationship long before my troubles could be named one through ten and I was naming them on a regular. When my life was at peace I believed in the God that made water wet, or created that breeze that you can only feel but never find, that turned a liquid into life and assigned death as a traveling companion when He called your breath home. For so many reasons, I believed in God but that belief didn't always coincide with the days of church attendance. When I was asked that question I was feeling guilty about my slacking church attendance. In time, as in the time I was praying for the food I think I had gotten over that guilt and could say with pride, "Yes I have a personal relationship with God." It would be this conviction I would use when asking for future help.

In this hour of need there were several days left of my one-hundred-and-fifty-mile roundtrip a day before payday. I didn't know how we were going to manage to the end of the week, I was just certain that somehow we would. With my thoughts on the empty cabinets, I remember driving home from work planning my strategy with God. When I get home, I will smoke a cigarette (that was when I smoked) take a minute to rest and then we, God, and I, would go out and find food somewhere, somehow. Where I was going I didn't have a clue but I was certain before the night was over we would have enough if I had to look under rocks to get it, I wouldn't come home without food. This plan of action was still on my mind as I pulled in the driveway and met my children as they ran to the car. Each one was screaming louder than the other about the food I left on the porch. "What food? I was just getting home," I explained to them "and I certainly didn't have any money to go shopping for food." Well if I didn't, who did? They wanted to know. They didn't want to know too badly. Even before I arrived home they had started eating the food. They were simply happy there was a lot of food to fill up the empty shelf space.

This mystery food delivery continued for weeks until one day I found out it was my neighbor, a Vietnam Veteran (probably who had served with my ex-husband) was bringing the food. He was unable to live a normal life inside a house after the war so he lived in the woods almost in front of my home. He would go to the supermarket just before the store closed and we all became happy recipients of a state Health Department Law. Meat products and dairy products that were removed from the refrigerated areas for a period of time could not be returned to the refrigerated area. They wouldn't stay out long enough to be spoiled, only long enough to violate a health law. Dented cans could not be sold but they could be given away. Boxed foods that looked damaged were not sold either. Other items with an expiration date of one or two days were also given away. The grocery stores gave out bags of food in the afternoon of items with up to date expirations and undamaged boxes also.

My Vietnam neighbor may not have been comfortable enough to live inside a home but he was physically fit enough to push a shopping cart two miles with enough bagged food for him, my other neighbor, and my family with whom he generously shared. My neighbor did not eat her food because she said she didn't know where it came from. I on the other hand had no idea who brought it but I was clear on who sent it. Every time I said my grace I gave Him thanks.

My children and I stayed in our home for some time after the food started coming and it continued. Gallons of milk, juice, rice, canned fruits, vegetables, meat, crackers, chips, basically a regular grocery list of food continued to be found on the porch. In hindsight, it could have been laced with arsenic but I knew it was not harmful to us. We ate our stomachs full even from the beginning when I wasn't sure who had delivered the food because I was confident that God had sent it.

One day Mr. Jenkins knocked on my door and asked for water. I brought him into the kitchen and filled his container. Then we went outside and I showed him where the faucet was and told him he was welcomed to water anytime. If we were not home he could get it from there and as much as he required anytime. As he was beginning to leave he turned around and asked me about the food on my porch. I was surprised to discover it was him, one because he didn't have a car for such deliveries and I saw him at such odd times I just never thought he was the one. But I went on to thank him and let him know what a God sent blessing he had been to my family. He was the food stamps I was never going to qualify for because I made 82 cents over the federal limit. It's interesting how that works, the working poor are not poor enough, but the never have worked qualify. I don't knock anyone's hustle but I know single mothers who genuinely struggle to pay bills and food stamps would balance their budget faster than a pay raise if they could get a little help from the system they pay taxes into. Then on the other hand there are the single mothers who make no effort to achieve anything other than learning the rules and regulations from Social Service and reap the benefits too often of this outstanding learning. But back to Mr. Jenkins, I thanked him and told him again how much he helped me and my family and told him if there was anything he ever wanted we were there for him.

The answer to my porch food was delivered in sprinting style fashion but the layout was filled with layers that I routinely use to remind myself how prayers work. Often, I've heard sermons on subjects like, your needs didn't catch God by surprise. God knew I was a single parent. He knew I had gotten that marriage thing all wrong and it left me with more consequences than conclusions. The surprise in my story was to accept that I wasn't going to be able to handle any of this life on my own. We take things into our own hands and plan a strategy that we think is designed to bring the best outcome. What we do last, is call upon God and wait to be instructed. In other words we fail to initially use God as our GPS, we get lost, frustrated, and waste time. Fortunately, we can get redirected when we accept we are going the wrong way.

Over the years, before and after this event, I have been the recipient of many answered prayers that were all delivered in different times, and some not answered the way I had hoped. I learned the lessons, regrouped, and moved forwarded armed with new and improved armor. This event, however, left me with an up close and personal review of the process and a reminder that my condition had not caught God by surprise. It was 5pm closing that I re-upped my petition for food assistance. I was feeling quite desperate and had submitted to the "whatever it takes" part to the prayer. "Dear God, if you say it's under the rock, under the rock is where I will look." It was there that I rested my case. My children had arrived home around 3:30 pm from school and discovered the food on the porch. This was a time long before beepers or cell phones or the children would have called and I could have stopped praying. I pulled into the driveway a little before 7pm by which time a good portion of the food was in digestive mode in the stomachs of my children. For the slow to learn, often like myself, the food was delivered around noon before I started praying. I guess that is the true example of manifestation.

I didn't wake up that morning a single parent and Mr. Jenkins had not moved onto his land the night before. People, places, and things had been arranged in such a way that we could be of use to each other. We both had needs and each would serve to provide for the other. Mr. Jenkins was the living example that God doesn't show up on your steps in the spirit. His spirit lives in the hearing and obedient actions of others. Whispered orders can easily fall upon ears God assigns to carry his plan through and often both parties become beneficiaries of the prayer request. I hope that Mr. Jenkins also knew that we were eternally grateful for his contributions and he will forever be remembered in my heart and spoken of in my stories as the deliverer of our porch food.

To Mr. Richard Jenkins and all the Veterans may they find the peace they deserve, God bless.

A SOMEDAY PLACE
Chapter Nine

The idea of a "someday place" visited me in 1976 one very cold, very snowy day in Grand Central Station, in NYC. It was not an earth-shattering revelation, rather a quiet and profound. I didn't know it then but later discovered it was a visitation of my inner spirit. It told me and kept me, but most of all, the idea of having a "someday place" saved me. It could be called a lot of things, but I think it is best described as hope on lay-a-way. Fortunately, it has no expiration date so it will remain there until you are able to pick it up.

A someday place is where dreams are held until you will execute them or dare to share. It is that place that everyone slinks to, without knowing it, each time someone dashes a hot burning dream with their dirty ice water. Often times, people are afraid your dreams might come true and they couldn't stand to see that happen. Other times, they just don't have the ability to hope when hopelessness is their constant daily companion. Their intent may not be genuinely hateful, but it cast a shadow over your world anyway. It is on all of these occasions that a private and secret place needs to be established. Then, there are those occasions when you feel that every single thing you touch turns to dust before your very eyes. Too many occasions have left you standing asking yourself, "How did I ever get in this hell and when will I ever get out?" The inward, personal condemnations are often the most harmful. The many disappointments of life can leave you breathless if you are not careful. Without a place that can hold and guard your hope filled dreams, you stand a good chance of turning into dust and blowing away with your dreams. So to recap, a someday place is a holder of dreams not yet realized, you can send them there. They will be safe, God will hold your key, and he's not judging.

My first memory of creating such a place dated back to when I was a small girl while living with Aunt Sis Rena. I can't be sure if I discovered it on my own or if a little girl had that inner spirit help. Aunt Sis Rena saved my life, she saved my soul but was unable to apply much or any physical affection to her daily routine of teaching.

In her defense, her heart spilled over with caring intent but rarely did these intensions rise to occasions of a physical display. Like myself she had been victim to too much of the ugly of life's unfolding. She had buried a husband, lost five hundred acres of land through thievery, buried a sister who died abruptly and another that was pulled out of the Cape Fear River. To say she was suffering from life's unfolding under-minded the true condition of her heart. I had an advantage that she didn't have. I was still young. There were lots I forgot and replaced with better memories, while she apparently was stuck in a place with too much reality. It was extremely late in her life for such a someday place. Her realities required a level of forgiveness she never reached. She loved me and she loved her cats. As I grew older, I learned her cats and a needy little girl, even without physical emotions, was her saving grace. Even though she never said it in those words, I heard it come in different ways.

On occasions her dormant emotions spilled over in a form of tears on Sunday. Rarely, did she get angry and I was always comforted by her words, because they stood for something. But a little girl, such as myself, who had seen so much and experienced so many abrupt losses before coming to live with her; I just craved more. I wanted hugs so tight, they took my breath. I wanted a kiss like a cool breeze on the top of my head that screams I love you without lips ever parting. But the more I tried to inch my way to make that happen the more I was turned away. She did not use harsh tones or ugly words but whatever was said, made it clear that I had barked up the wrong tree. Once, at ten or eleven, I remembered feeling out of sorts. We were sitting on the davenport (now called a couch), and I moved to lay my head in her lap. She moved my head and suggested that I go to one of my two rooms if I wanted to lie down. We had a three-bedroom house and it was only the two of us. Every two or three months I got bored and necessitated a relocation so I rearranged the other room to move in it. While that was always fun, neither the move nor the room served as substitution for physical affection. Eventually, I stopped. I didn't stop desiring hugs, I accepted they would not come from her and I resolved, if not then, one day. Still she had her way about her. Like the day I got caught in the thunderstorm and arrived like the cavalry.

She knew I'd be standing outside on my way to school looking like a crazy wet chicken after the great storm. That was the hugs and kisses. It was on such occasions I wallowed around in the wonderfulness of that attention, even if I wanted more attention. It was during such times that I created of a someday place. Someday I'd have hugs and kisses. Someday it would be alright to extend my arm and hug someone as they arrived or departed. Just wait. She had no way of knowing, nor did I, that she was really helping me create a diversion from immediate troubles. I was learning to extend a very long arm of faith to trust while developing an ability to hold on. One day, no matter what I was going through, that day delivered me to a better day. It was those thoughts that rushed through my head on one very cold New York winter. Someday I will be better dressed and warm standing in this same spot.

Before global warming and other weather condition phenomena, New York winters could be clearly defined by temperatures. True winter started around Thanksgiving. Weather temperatures dropped from November to December and settled for several weeks between eight and fifteen degrees, Christmas was always white. Often the forecast sounded out a wind chill factor alarm of eight to ten degrees below zero, and a stay in advisory was given. Snowflakes fell routinely and inches added up to feet that came to rest well over the tops of many benches. There was no state of alarm or milk and bread sold out because everyone had stacked up already. Winter never took anyone by surprise, it arrived and people accepted it. This was a time when fur and leather coats were factored into fashion as it was as necessary to be warm as it was to be cute. Store fronts in all boroughs advertised their wear at competing prices because it was understood that no matter who you bought from; you were going to buy somewhere. Although the buying was a given, that was often my problem. Winter didn't catch me by surprise either, but it caught me with more ends to meet than rope to make it happen. So often, this realization lived out in an underdressed wait in the Grand Central Station.

Grand Central Station is one of New York City's busiest

subway stations located at 42nd Street and Park Avenue. The daily commuter numbers could reach between 250,000 daily and many more during the holidays. It sounds like an outrageous number, but if ever you were physically in the station at rush hour, you could easily be swept up by the busy exchanges and believe the numbers. Commuters arrive by bus or train, getting on and off, headed somewhere; anxiously desiring a safe and speedy trip. Some headed up-town to Harlem, some to New Haven, downtown to the village or Wall Street areas, or to the Staten Island Ferry. Many maybe waiting for a train to go directly to their destination, others would be rushing for a transfer that would add another hour to their already two-hour daily commute.

My commute home averaged an hour if there were no train delays and took me on a less busy side of Grand Central. I worked for Philip Morris which was across the street from the train station entrance and the neighborhood was inhabited by individuals on all financial levels. The consideration of such financial success often pinched me as I passed the office of Liberty Travel and observed the many winter get away travel advertisements. The images lived on in my heart as I faded into the many steps that delivered me down to the Number 7 Train, arrival to the Borough of Queens.

The 80's was also a good economic year for many who had planned better than me who could afford the many trips advertised by the travel agency. In the spring, I found a seat or wait for a seat to empty out. There I sat and wondered what fabulous travel arrangements were in the making at Liberty Travel. In the winter, I entertained that same thought but to my travel dreams I added warm boots, a winter coat with hats and gloves to match. Not just for world travel but daily travel with destinations within the scope of one hour.

The day I called up my "someday place" was such a winter day. The sidewalks were filled with newly fallen and frozen snow while the streets were filled with icy slush caused by the cars and cabs which busied the streets. There was no way for me to avoid stepping in puddles of melting ice while attempting to cross the street to the train stations. By the time I reached the very short distance, my feet were soaked and the cold was setting in. There was nothing to do but be cold with the understanding I was going to be cold for the entire commute. Once I reached the final platform on this day I just wanted to burst into tears. Where did I go wrong? How did this happen and when would I get out of life's hole? I found a place I could rest myself against so I could take turns holding one foot up then the other trying to get warm. It didn't work. I stood feeling absolutely hopeless. Then I remembered the "why" and "how." The why I was cold with boots not prepared to meet New York City winters was simple. I had three small children and my numbers were not adding up. Once upon a time that sentence included a husband, some children, and shared responsibilities. That would have left a few dollars for a good pair of boots and maybe even a warm coat. Lately, my life had experienced seriously bad subtraction acts. One less adult and even less money divided by three small children did not equal much warm clothes for mommy. Momentarily I felt defeated and I placed both my feet on the platform and leaned my entire weight against the partition. If so many people had not been around I might have cried out loud. However, since there were so many commuters I had good moments for observation with lots of fashion thoughts for my future hopes.

    This much constant activity provided me with an array of styles, colors, and shapes for me to wish upon as I stood next to the steps on the platform. I can't say with accuracy how many people were on the platform waiting for the same #7 train to Flushing, but four or five hundred would not have been in excess. The platform is very long and is divided in the middle with dark wooden benches. By the time I arrived on the platform all the seats had been taken, but not to worry a train would come in, people would scurry to get closer for the next train and empty a row of seats. But I did not rush, nor scurry. I rested against the stairwell that provided the most heat and had plans to remain in that exact spot until my train arrived. Surely, there would be some pushing and shoving because I would not be standing right at the train door upon its arrival but I was prepared for that. Anyway, my feet were frozen and I had to have time for blood to find its way down. Also, I had the misfortunate opportunity of observing a passenger fall onto the platform once and learned that several rows from the train door would be fine. The commuters would push you in anyway.

    So there I was standing, observing, and thawing out some. Commuters hurried down the steps. Some were securely wrapped in some animal fur that some advocacy group would later blast about animal cruelty. They will probably be wearing leather shoes when they do it. There were nice wool coats of assorted colors and styles many with hats, gloves, and scarves to match. Absolutely no shivering was observed as I watched the commuters come and go and it was then I was revisited by the lay-away spirit of someday. I leaned against the stairwell and envisioned a day when I would return, I would still be one of the 250,000 busy on my way to somewhere, but, I was going to be warm. I was going to be warm in nice warm boots that were new when I bought them and were sized accurately to suit my feet. The coat probably wouldn't be fur, not because I care about the animal activist but because I'm allergic to fur. It would be wool, dyed in a color to fit my desire and measured appropriately to fit my size. The visions of my someday place were disrupted as the train pulled in and tired commuters began to buzz all around me. It was alright because I would be on the train in minutes and would find heat to position my feet next to. Once I was off the train it would be minutes before a bus arrived and shortly after that I would be home. There were some little people that needed to be raised and a lot more poorly dressed cold days before I would return to Grand Central Station. But I was on my way.

Everyone is born with great purpose and intension. Artist, politicians, educators, spiritual leaders, medical professionals we are all seeded with the life for achievement. This life can seep out if not kept, protected, and stored properly. As adverse life conditions challenge your hopes, find a place where they are kept and there is no judgment. A *'someday place'* will serve you well and no one even has to know.

THE END OF A SEASON
Chapter Ten

My humble beginnings did not begin in the town of Fayetteville, NC It was the now overpriced gentrified neighborhood of Bedford-Stuyvesant in Brooklyn, NY, AKA Bed Stuy. A house in the three hundred block of Green Street housed my parents and siblings. Once a family of five lived with high hopes and at that count that number had not yet included me. I would arrive three years after the death of a brother born before me and three years before a sister who would arrive on Independence Day. We, like all families no matter their social or economic status began our lives with sets of thoughts only to always be redirected because of time and circumstance. Some fare better than others while many get lost in the transition never to find the paths of their original plan. Mother's death served as a serious redirection for my entire family but I was fortunate to have been picked up during my transition. A collection of miscellaneous home address would serve as a bridge to where I finally resided and helped to make me thankful for family.

The safe house of the unpainted color of brown became my home address for an eleven-year stay. It rested on the outskirts of the city limits where life revolved around seasons. Farmers planted in one season and harvest began in another season. This lifestyle kept me thoughtful of how life unfolds and made me view my life in acts of seasons. "For everything there is a season", became my daily bread. Although it was not hammered into my head through words, it was indeed securely planted through actions.

The first season of my life was the get started phase. It was a part of things that fall apart and then becoming an active participate of the restoration. In this position I was taught of the finer things of life, love, hope and faith. They would become the key components of my existence as I grew from child to young adult. Life experiences routinely tested me and I failed as much as I passed. Each failure gave me new insights and the opportunity to get stronger in an area that had fallen short and there were many. I learned the hard way that things happen as much without planning as they do with intent. And it is usually the ones that lacked planning that will take the longest to repair.

I was approaching thirty by the time I returned home and brought with me the consequences of my life's actions. I was twice married, once divorced with three small children in my image. From any point of view it all looked like real life and it was. I had been taught the benefits of prayer and faith and so on but until my aunt's death it was learned information not used. It would be after her death that the test would come hard and fast like labor and I had to give way to becoming a quick learner. The season of my youth had its challenges but was filled with memories with promises to keep me. There were no gifts more precious than my children whether planned or not they were the true wind beneath my wings. Some single parents would think that children blew them down, not mine. My children blew me onward, and I loved them even more. They helped me hear the whispers of, it's going to be alright and we're going to make it.

I, like a good farmer at the end of a season arrived at the place of inventory. I would review my earnings, acknowledge my mistakes, and prepare to plant a new crop based on past information. Soon I would be leaving the town of Fayetteville

Wilderness Places

for sights unknown and experiences yet to live. There were no certainties but there was a lot of hope. My developing years represented a season of healing and learning. I had been assigned to a garden as a broken seed and even as a student of life. There I was nourished, healed, and taught. All of that would be the backdrop of future travels and achievements.

My adult stay in the house on Ingram Street informed me that I did not have a personal relationship with God but it was something I would seek out. This search would not be to satisfy any one of the many religions I had opportunities to witness. It would be to satisfy a yearning I was missing and probably not to be found from the pew of a church. As a child I grew to love the mystery of nature and felt that the God spirit was so active in places and things that we could not contain. With this child's heart I learned the answer to a hardship could be found in obedience. Miracles really do happen and were found in grocery bags skillfully placed on the porch of a desperate single mother. A Vietnam Veteran, who resided in the woods could receive immediate gratification from delivering that food and maybe forget for a moment what war had been. I learned that if you really seek you can find and an earthly job rejected equals a spiritual promotion received, a yes, you're hired, is waiting in the wings. I learned not to think too hard on how the miracle would come, such as the porch food, but trust the process of the miracle and receive it when it arrived.

For that and so much more, I gave thanks as I planted new seeds to become the more seasons in my life's journey.

See you at the next market.

ABOUT THE AUTHOR

Marche Hilton Singleton is an African American activist, published author, of prose and poetry, and a public speaker. She fell in love with words early in life and attempted to turn them into something that matter. Her writings focus on the daily bread of life. That covers many aspects of the human existence and condition.

An upbringing in a Jim Crow South of the fifties molded her reality, but the love of a close knit Black community helped to give way to happy endings. She was raised by her mother's oldest sister whose father was Irish and had the joy of her grandmother's love. Her skin shined with the hue of the blue/black that's found among the Sudanese people of Africa. Her father was a rare item in her life and she would learn later that his father had arrived in the US by way of Trinidad. Life lessons taught her that no matter how much of a hodgepodge of blood ran in her veins, she would be her grandmother's child, live life and report it accordingly. Religion played an important role in her childhood, but as she aged it would lean more towards God and less towards the many interpretations of the written word delivered by the church. As an eternal optimist, she delivers her many stories with honesty and concludes her sentences with a dash of hope that leaves the reader willing to start the next story.

www.ingramcontent.com/pod-product-compliance
Lightning Source LLC
Chambersburg PA
CBHW062027290426
44108CB00025B/2810